# SCHOOL-AGE IDEAS
# AND ACTIVITIES
# FOR
# AFTER SCHOOL PROGRAMS

## BY KAREN HAAS-FOLETTA AND MICHELE COGLEY

## ILLUSTRATED BY MARY R. THOMASON

## PHOTOS BY CHRIS POWELL

PUBLISHED BY School-Age NOTES
1990

## Acknowledgements

We would like to thank Karen's mother, Carolyn Buhai Haas, who is the co-author of *I Saw a Purple Cow*, *A Pumpkin in a Pear Tree*, *Children are Children are Children*, *Backyard Vacation*, *Purple Cow to the Rescue!*, and author of *The Big Book of Fun* and *Look at Me*. She helped with ideas and editing of the book.

We would also like to thank the Parent Board, staff and children at West Portal Center For After School Recreation and Education (C.A.R.E.). This is where our ideas and activities are tested and proven successful. We are also grateful to Linda Tanimasa for her assistance in the indoor/outdoor games section.

Michele would like to thank all the teachers and master teachers who have shared their expertise and creativity with her.

Published by:

# School-Age NOTES

A National Resource Organization on School–Age Care

**For a free resource catalog write to:**

School-Age NOTES
P.O. Box 40205
Nashville, TN 37204
(615) 242-8464

Library of Congress Catalog Card Number: 90-63115

10  9  8  7  6  5

ISBN: 0-917505-03-4

This book has been printed on 50% recycled paper.

Every 1000 copies of this book printed on this recycled paper
saves 6 mature trees.

To our husbands,
Jon Foletta and Paul Cogley
and our children
Nicholas Foletta born January 11, 1989
Chris and Azrael Bigler and Matthew and Nathaniel Cogley

# CONTENTS

# INTRODUCTION

Caring for school-age children during their out-of-school hours is a profession requiring a unique mix of skills and abilities on the part of the adult leaders. This book was written for directors and staff of school-age care programs. The ideas and suggestions may also be valuable for elementary school teachers, preschool programs, family day care providers, recreation programs, scouting groups, baby sitters, and parents of school-age children.

Even though there are many activity and informational books on the market, it is often difficult to determine which ideas and projects work best for school-age children. When we talked with numerous people involved in school-age care, it became clear that there is still a great need for a practical, straight-forward, age-appropriate informational and activity guide. As directors of before-and-after school programs, we have used the ideas, suggestions, and activities in this book successfully with school-age children for several years. Our ideas come from many sources including books and magazines, conferences, workshops, university class work, other child care workers, and from real life experiences. Although some of the activities are "old standards," they are included because school-age children enjoy them. *Whenever we share experiences that have happened at our center the words are italicized.*

## Changes Necessary In Our Profession

Unlike preschool, school-age care has in the past been a scattered, unorganized, and isolated profession. As stated in the School-Age Child Care Project Newsletter (SACC), "Although thousands of programs now exist across the country, where a few years ago there were only hundreds, there are still many communities where school-age child care is at best a dream, and many communities where program staff, administrators, and school-age child care folks rarely get together in an organized way."[1]

Many providers feel frustrated by the lack of training, support and professionalism in this field. Recruiting and retaining qualified, experienced staff that meet the needs of school-age children are major concerns. Low pay, part-time hours, and lack of recognition make it difficult for concerned personnel to stay committed.

Few college courses are devoted to training school-age child care professionals. Although somewhat helpful, current elementary education, child development, and early childhood education course work does not focus on the special requirements of the after school situation. School-age children's developmental needs and interests are very different than those of preschool children. School-age child care is not a continuation of academic classroom experiences or adult-directed activities. Nancy P. Alexander writes, "After-school care involves aspects of elementary education, recreation, social service, family relations, and child development....Currently far too few staff training programs are designed to meet the special needs of school-age children in care."[2]

## Change Is Coming

Lack of professional training and recognition is slowly giving way to increased public awareness. There are over a dozen states where active groups have been formed. For example, in Ohio there is an organization called Professionals for School-Age Child Care and in Minnesota, the School-Age Child Care Alliance. California has the oldest and largest group of its kind, the California School Age Consortium (CSAC). CSAC was organized in 1982 and presents a yearly school-age child care and recreation conference which is the largest in the nation. These groups provide support services, newsletters, training and legislative lobbying for school-age programs. National leadership of the field

---

1. Michelle Seligson, "Keeping in Touch," SACC Newsletter, Vol. 4, July 1987, p.2.

2. Nancy P. Alexander, "School-Age Child Care: Concerns and Challenges," Young Children, Nov. 1986, p. 7

of school-age care has been provided by the School-Age Child Care Project at Wellesley College, funded since 1979, and by School-Age NOTES, a national resource organization established in 1980. Both groups have provided written materials, training, and technical assistance which have formed the foundation of our field. The National Association for the Education of Young Children (NAEYC) has a school-age track as part of its national conference and has published books and articles addressing school-age issues. The National School-Age Child Care Alliance (SACCA) was formed in November of 1987. This group networks the state and local groups together on a national level.

All school-age programs are different depending on population, number of children, space, facility, type of program, staff training and leadership. In spite of these differences, people who work with children share an ultimate goal of helping all children develop to their fullest potential. Although individual organizations have different names, they are united in their goals for increasing both the number of school-agers receiving care and the quality of care. Training of school-age care staff, increasing public awareness of the need, and advocating in local and state governments are a part of the work that must be done by school-age child care professionals now and in the future.

**What To Call Ourselves**

Throughout this book you will read many names used to describe the adults who take care of school-age children during their out-of-school hours. *In our program we have a Director who runs the entire program, an Assistant Director who is second in charge and runs the program when the director is absent, teachers and teachers' aides.* The licensing agency in California calls school-age care providers teacher/director, teachers and aides. In some states they are not allowed to be called teachers unless they are academic teachers working in a classroom. Being considered professionals is very important. School-age caregivers are not baby sitters, nor custodial care providers. We feel strongly that although we are not teachers in the formal academic sense, and our curriculum is not adult-directed, we *do* teach the children a variety of important skills. Thus, we have decided to use the word "teacher" in this text. We also use the words "adult leader," "staff member," "caregiver," and "child care professional."

Richard Scofield, Editor/Publisher of School-Age NOTES, states, "We may continue to call our individual programs and job titles by different names. However, let us declare ourselves and band together as professionals who care for and about school-agers."[3]

---

3.Richard Scofield, "What's in a name???" *School-Age NOTES*, May/June 1989 VOL IX, p. 2

# PHILOSOPHY

Children spend many hours in out-of-school care. It is their "home away from home" and is a place where a great deal of growth and development takes place. All children need to develop a sense of belonging in their care facility.

The safety of the children is critical! Structure and limits are necessary to avoid chaos. Clearly posted safety rules, which the children can help develop, allow children to know what is expected of them. It is essential that rules are enforced consistently, and that children know what the consequences are for breaking them. If the children feel safe and secure, they will feel free to select and pursue activities that hold their interest. Many school-age children equate limits with love. If there are no limits placed upon them they may feel neglected and act out inappropriately.

Within the structure and limits, there needs to be much freedom and many choices. **Free play activities** should be a central part of out-of-school care programs. The children's diverse needs, interests, and developmental levels need to be taken into account when developing curriculum. The environment should be designed to be challenging, both mentally and physically, to foster independence, and to allow children to grow and develop at their own rate.

Input into the program content by both parents and children is vital. **In other words, it should be the children's program.** Parents want to feel that their concerns for their children are being met. While child care professionals offer valuable experience, their role is primarily that of facilitator. It is their responsibility to strive to meet the group and individual needs of all the children and their families.

The key ingredient to a successful program is a well-rounded staff. School-agers do not want staff to treat them like preschoolers. They also do not want the same structure as in elementary school. To be effective school-age caregivers, staff members must adapt and expand their backgrounds in early childhood education or elementary education to give appropriate care to school-age children. Training in recreation, physical education and specialties such as art or music contribute to a well rounded staff.

# ROOM ARRANGEMENT

## Programs With Exclusive Space

Programs which have "dedicated" space, not shared with any other program are very fortunate. Room arrangement is critical for a successful program. Arranging the environment is an ever-changing process. What works one year may not prove effective the next. When planning indoor environments, keep in mind the interests and developmental levels of the children.

A common approach to room arrangement is learning centers or activity areas. *This is the approach we have found to be the most successful in our programs.* These areas include prepared environments where children have options to choose activities depending on their interests. There is free flow from one area to the next. Children do not have to ask permission to be in an area of the room and they choose how long to stay at a project. Thus, if Mary wants to spend her entire free play time playing a game and Jimmy wants to do several activities, both are acceptable. If a child has trouble finding something to do, a teacher assists by verbalizing the choices available, but lets the child make his or her own decision.

Some programs have children rotate from one center to the next, for a set time period. These programs are more teacher oriented than the free flow types. Other centers will change or alternate moveable activity areas on a daily or weekly basis.

When creating the room arrangement there are several factors to keep in mind:

1. Safety factors such as clear fire exits.

2. The traffic patterns in and around areas.

3. Size and location of each interest area.

4. Placement of areas, such as separating noisy activities from quiet places.

5. Distribution of areas to facilitate movement of children from one area to another.

6. Arrangement of interest areas to allow for adequate adult supervision and visibility through the use of low shelves, room dividers, bookcases, and couches.

7. Access to sinks for art, science and cooking.

8. Close proximity to bathrooms and drinking fountains.

9. Sufficient storage for supplies and equipment.

The environment should include the following areas if possible:

1. **A quiet, soft area** — with sofa, bean bags, carpet or rug, and books situated away from doors or high traffic patterns. It is designed for reading, quiet games, relaxing, storytelling, and privacy. An old bathtub filled with pillows makes a great reading place.

2. **An open area for group or circle time** — with a rug or carpet squares, large enough to accommodate the whole group without discomfort.

3. **An area for block building** — construction and other fine motor skills. This area may include a complete block set (hollow as well as unit blocks), Legos™, cars and trucks, bristle blocks™, flexible blocks, plastic animals, people, etc. Blocks are a very important part of play and math development!

4. **An area for dress-up and dramatic play** — school-age children are

4

developing work patterns and are interested in work of all sorts. They want to have real items such as: pots, pans, dishes and tools. This area can be changed into: a post office, an office, a beauty parlor, a doctor's office, a shoe or clothing store, or grocery store. Place items for each idea in large labeled boxes that can be easily stored and reused.

5. **An area for game playing and storage** — Include in this area a variety of games, horizontal surfaces for game playing, open space for floor games, puzzles and other manipulatives. Make sure storage space is well labeled with ample space for games of different sizes and shapes. Without organization this area can be very messy! Store pieces for games and puzzles in zip-lock™ bags or plastic tubs with lids. The plastic bags can be hung from a string with clothespins. Label the backs of puzzle pieces so that lost pieces can be easily returned to the right puzzle.

6. **An area for hands-on science and nature exploration** — with a science table or area accessible to all children. A shelf above the table is excellent for things to be looked at and not touched. However, the majority of items should be hands on. This area can also include pictures, posters, and maps. (See the Science Section for more information.)

7. **An older children's area** — a special spot just for the older children. (See the section on Older Children for more ideas.)

8. **An art area** — with ample storage space to provide for both individual and group activities. Include materials that are easily accessible and are always available for use by the children such as plenty of paper, crayons, tape, scissors, glue, scrap material, yarn, and paper plates. Limit the stacks of paper to avoid over-usage and unnecessary mess. Store materials for special projects in a place that will be inaccessible to the children. Shelves for unfinished projects are also desirable. A multi-sided easel with a vinyl mat underneath and a drying rack are wonderful for painting. If possible, set up a table just for clay projects. Good lighting and separation from the general traffic flow is important. (See the Arts and Crafts Sections for more suggestions.)

9. **A cubbie area** — where children can store their belongings. Children need a place to hang their coats and store their personal things. Traditional cubbies can be purchased, or you can be innovative by stacking items such as plastic crates.

10. **A lockable storage area** — for supplies and equipment as well as staff's belongings.

11. **A cooking area** — for preparation and storage of food and utensils for snack time.

12. **A parent area** — with sign-in/out sheets, mailboxes, folders to store children's finished art work which is ready to take home, and a bulletin board.

13. **A staff area** — with staff mailboxes, a place to store belongings, a bulletin board with emergency procedures, staff information and schedules posted, and a reference library. If possible a staff lounge area is wonderful for those moments when breaks are feasible. This should include a coffee or tea pot, comfortable chairs and a telephone.

**Programs with Shared Space**

Unfortunately, many programs do not have the luxury of a space to call their own. However, with imagination, creativity, and organization, it is possible to provide a quality program in shared space. The key to this process is having plenty of lockable storage units so that equipment can be easily and safely wheeled in and out.

- Interest areas can still be set up on a daily basis.

- Shelves with wheels can be utilized for each area.

- Large pillows and bean bag chairs can substitute for heavier quiet-area furniture.

- Portable signs, bulletin boards on wheels and backs of shelves can be used to define and label the learning centers and serve as room dividers.

- Pegboard is versatile. It is excellent for hanging things, making room dividers, and enclosing areas for privacy.

- Art supplies can be stored on wheeled shelves, containers such as baskets, large cans and tins, covered ice cream tubs or chicken buckets, and shoe boxes.

- Removable carpet squares can be used for the quiet and group sections because they are easily stacked.

- Plastic stackable containers on wheels work for movable cubbies.

- The use of "spill over space," such as a hall and special rooms, is great for doing small group projects.

Many programs are not allowed to put anything on the walls. To display children's art work or put up posters, drape material, sheets, oil cloths or plastic pieces over the walls. (Check with fire safety regulations first.) Large chalk boards, cork boards and foam boards on wheels can be purchased. Portable room dividers are available from office supply catalogs.

Programs with exclusive space may still, in many cases, have some shared space. *In our program we have a large room to call our own but also share the use of the school library and the auditorium.* When sharing any space, develop a mutually acceptable plan with whomever the space is being shared. *In our situation, by working together with the school librarian and principal, we have a sharing situation that does not cause problems. This, however, did take time and flexibility to develop. We asked the school librarian, and staff what they needed us to do in order to share their space. Our mutually acceptable plan includes keeping the shared space neat and clean, storing our belongings and putting the furniture back to a prescribed set-up, daily.* Remember, in school-based programs the school principal, secretary and janitor can make or break a program. Getting on their good side, by communicating effectively and regularly, can prevent misunderstandings!

# WHAT OUR PROGRAM IS LIKE

*Many people ask us why our room arrangement works so successfully. A one major reason is our low adult-child ratio (1:10). We also have a large space which we divide into well defined interest areas. However, most importantly, our staff is dedicated to meeting the needs of school-age children. Many choices are built into a structured environment. Children decide what activity they wish to pursue. The following is a freeze-frame of what our center looks like during a typical, free play period. Free play, our free choice time, is the core of our curriculum. Free choice works for us because the planned interest areas, although often continuously changing, structure the environment.*

**Free Play Time**

*It is 4:30 p.m. There are 65 children present. They already have had an outdoor time, eaten snack and have done their homework. It is now free choice time both indoors and outdoors.*

*QUIET AREA — Two girls play the piano. On the rug three children are holding animals (our pet rat, guinea pig and rabbit). One child, sitting on a bean bag chair, reads a book. Sprawled on the couch, two children are trading stickers. Three boys have set-up the wooden train set on the rug.*

*ART AREA — At the art table six children and one teacher are making baskets. Two other children are cutting and pasting pictures and two are making pictures of space ships.*

*GAME AREA — Two children challenge each other with checkers while one enjoys watching the game.*

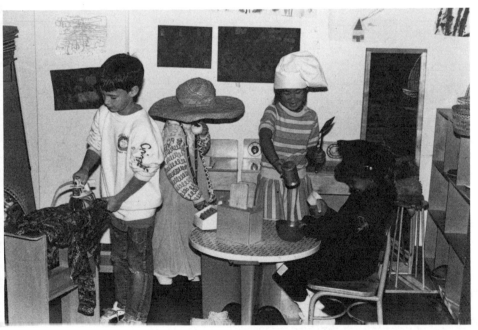

*DRESS-UP — Putting on adult-sizes clothes, three girls and a boy are absorbed in playing house.*

*THE THIRD GRADE AREA — Five youngsters recreate an office. They divide themselves into roles as president, secretary, vice-president and general office workers. Mats have been propped with signs saying "third graders only". Nearby, a staff member and a child play a board game.*

*BLOCK AREA — A large structure has been erected out of wooden blocks by three "builders". They have positioned the largest blocks so that others will not knock down their work.*

*SCIENCE TABLE — Three butterflies, just as they hatch out of their cocoons, capture the attention of one six year old.*

*OLDER CHILDREN'S ROOM — Across the hall in the library, two preadolescents sketch on drawing pads. Two others play a game; one continues working on his homework.*

*OUTSIDE — In the play yard, 20 children are involved in various activities, including hopping on a pogo ball, playing dodge ball, playing a mini-tennis game, and jumping rope.*

*The eight staff members present are strategically spaced throughout both indoor and outdoor areas. One is in the library with her group, four are in the main room, two are watching children outdoors, and one is in the kitchen cleaning up snack.*

# MULTICULTURAL CURRICULUM

Before planning a multicultural curriculum, it is vital to look at the population your school serves, the community in which the school exists and the United States as a whole. Also explore the cultural background of your staff. During staff meetings or inservice training, discuss each staff member's cultural background. Every society or group has its own manner of doing things, including traditions, customs, practices, philosophy, behavior, language, communication, clothing and celebrations. This makes up culture and is learned rather than genetic. The culture that people grow up in tends to influence them strongly in areas such as child rearing practices, family roles, socialization patterns, values and religious beliefs.

Built within a culture are also biases or prejudices about other cultures. When developing a multicultural curriculum, discussion of staffs' cultural bias or prejudice is important. Talk about varying life styles, time concepts, and the values and beliefs of each staff member. Teachers must understand who they are and feel proud of their own cultural background before they are ready to assist children in learning about their own and other cultures.

Suzanne Dame, who is a Native American child advocate, says that the three most important aspects of teaching children about another culture are: be respectful, accurate, and authentic. For example, she does not feel that children should "play at being Indians" as if being an Indian is an occupation. Playing at being any race is disrespectful. Children need to learn to respect and explore similarities and cultural differences.

Parents need to be aware that your center is developing a multicultural curriculum and be made an integral part of the planning process. This could be done through newsletters, parent meetings or group discussions. Parents and extended families are excellent resources for multicultural activities and experiences. Ask parents to contribute items from their culture or share stories, recipes and folklore.

Louise Derman-Sparks in her book Anti-Bias Curriculum: Tools for Empowering Young Children tells about a very exciting new approach. She writes, "Anti-bias curriculum embraces an educational philosophy as well as specific techniques and content. It is value based: Differences are good; oppressive ideas and behaviors are not. It sets up a creative tension between respecting differences and not accepting unfair beliefs and acts."[4] She feels that most multicultural curricula have a positive goal, that of teaching children about other cultures, but do not address the important issues of everyday life of these cultures in America. She calls this a "tourist curriculum" which is based solely on studies of holidays, household items and foods. She writes, "Tourist curriculum is both patronizing, emphasizing the "exotic" differences between cultures, and trivializing, dealing not with the real-life daily problems and experiences of different people, but with surface aspects of their celebrations and modes of entertainment."[5] The book tells how to implement an anti-bias curriculum including activities, curriculum and parent involvement. It also deals with bias against people with disabilities and sexism.

Holidays are a good way to teach children about their own and other cultural experiences but should not be the main focus for the multicultural curriculum.

When choosing what holidays to incorporate into your curriculum, follow these suggestions:

- Find out what holidays *your children celebrate* and what special preparations, activities and ceremonies are involved.

- Provide children with a historically accurate background about the holiday.

---

4. Louise Derman-Sparks and the A.B.C. Task Force, *Anti-Bias Curriculum Tools for Empowering Young Children* (Washington, DC: National Association for the Education of Young Children, 1989), p. X

5. Ibid., p. 7

9

- Respect every holiday equally and do not treat one holiday as "exotic" and another as commonplace.

- Be aware that certain family beliefs do not allow participation in particular holiday celebrations. If this is the case in your center, work with the parents in creating acceptable alternatives for the child while the holiday observance is going on.

- Remember that low income families may find certain holidays stressful because of ever increasing financial expectations and commercialization.

When planning curriculum in school-age programs:

- Expose children to a variety of multicultural activities.

- Do not make the multicultural activities special events, but rather an ongoing part of everyday curriculum.

- Integrate activities throughout the learning centers or interest areas.

- Have a variety of items, not just one or two, about each culture, such as books, games, pictures, photographs, posters, dolls, music, musical instruments and puzzles.

- Reflect different nationalities through the use of art materials such as brown, black and tan paper, dough, crayons and collage materials.

- Use resources such as garage sales, restaurants, gift shops, and import shops in ethnic sections of cities, and the library to obtain items to incorporate in your curriculum.

It is important that items used for multicultural curriculum are not always about people living in other countries, but rather portray the different cultures living in the United States. Families with diverse cultural backgrounds, who live in the United States, act differently than those living in their native countries. Studies of people in other countries can be done as a separate unit of study or theme for each nation.

# PROGRAM SCHEDULING

Before they arrive at after school care, school-age children spend much of their day sitting and doing structured activities. After school is a time for exercise, socializing, eating snacks and making choices. The program must include a variety of activities geared to different age levels, interests, and abilities. Many parents require that their children do homework during child care. Ask parents individually to decide if they want homework done at child care; then abide by their requests. *We set aside a supervised time for homework, but do not allow children to spend long periods of time doing this work (for the younger children, 20 to 30 minutes and for older children, 45 minutes to an hour).*

Scheduling for after school programs is something that is very distinctive to each particular program. How the after school program is set up should be related to the type of elementary school program the children are in. For example, some elementary schools have structured academic time at the end of the day, others have a play period. Time constraints can also rapidly change program scheduling. If children get out of school after 3:30 p.m., they may need a snack right away. Make the schedule flexible; it may change from month to month or year to year according to the size, ages and the needs of the children.

Some suggestions for scheduling are:

1. Allow time for kindergarten children to rest.

2. First through fifth graders do not generally need a rest, but some still may want to sit and "do nothing" or lounge and read a book. Let children daydream after school.

3. Outside time is important when the children first arrive. After a long day of school, many children will feel oppressed if made to sit for quiet activities.

4. Limit a group "greeting" time to ten minutes and then let the children participate in large motor play and sports.

5. Set snack for a time when children seem hungry. *Between 3:00 and 4:00 p.m. works well for our program.* Some programs have "come and get it" type snacks; others have a sit-down snack.

6. Let each child help prepare and clean up snack at least every other week if possible; it is a great learning experience! Or set up snack in a manner which allows the children to participate by pouring, spreading, cutting and mixing.

7. Do homework after snack <u>and</u> after outdoor time when the children are not experiencing hunger pains and have released some of their extra energy.

8. Always include at least an hour of free play and art activities in the daily schedule.

9. Try to arrange professional lessons for interested students in areas such as dance, creative movement, music, drama, karate, or tennis. Many working parents appreciate this service, but the lessons must be at a reasonable cost.

10. Let the children help plan the schedule. Their input will indicate their needs and develop a sense of ownership to make the schedule work for them.

Two examples of schedules are the following:

| | Large programs *(50-100 children)* | Smaller programs |
|---|---|---|
| **12:00-2:40** | Kindergarten children only | |
| **12:00-12:30** | Lunch (kindergarten) | Lunch |
| **12:30-1:00** | Free play and art activities | Free play time |
| **1:00-1:30** | Story time and bathroom | Story time |
| **1:30-2:40** | Rest time, (non-sleepers may get up at 2:00) | Rest time |
| **2:40-3:00** | Group time (K-2nd grade) (outdoor time older children) | Outside time all children |
| **3:00-3:30** | Outdoor time (all children) One group prepares snack | Large group altogether (3:30-3:45) |
| **3:30-4:00** | Snack time by age group | |
| **3:45-4:00** | Group time (older children) | Snack all children |
| **4:00-4:30** | Homework/Free play for those without or who do not do, homework (By age group) | Activity/project time |
| **4:30-5:30** | Activity time free play both indoors and outdoors | Homework (4:30-5:00) Free play |
| **5:30-6:00** | Indoor quiet activities/ clean up | Indoor quiet activities |

# A CHANCE TO BE CHILDREN

Children's lives today are often over scheduled and hurried. Some parents fill up their children's free time with activities and put pressure on them to succeed. They are rushed from one endeavor to another, given little opportunity to just be themselves. There is a tendency for parents, teachers, peers, the media, and society in general to encourage children to grow up quickly. Children are frequently pushed past their important years into the adult world. They are encouraged to assume adult values toward clothing, sports, responsibilities, academics, adult problems, boy/girl relations, and commitment to future goals.

There is not a direct way to control the flow of adult-type information into their lives, but there are ways to help them find time to grow more naturally and at their own pace. Make your program the place where those hurried and pushed children can slow down. Permit children to find the time to have fun, relax, create, hang out, talk, share, explore, and just be kids. Let children even find the time to be "bored". Dr. David Elkind, the author of <u>The Hurried Child</u> [6] says that it is good for children to be bored, because then they have to go into themselves for their own resources. These days, too many children do not have a chance to reflect. After school programs are a perfect place for these moments of self-exploration to occur.

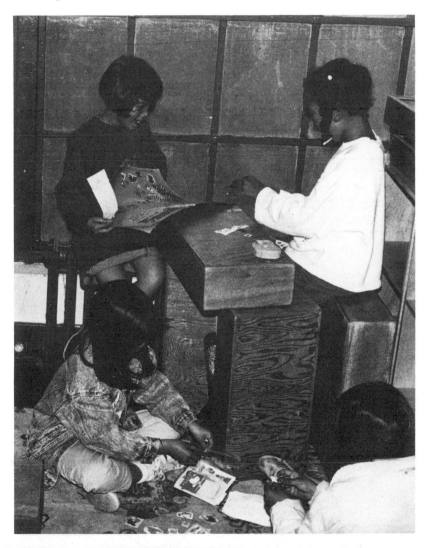

6. David Elkind, *The Hurried Child* (Reading MA. Addison- Wesley Publishing Co., 1988)

# LARGE GROUP TIME OR CIRCLE TIME

It is a good idea to have a time of day when all the children get together for a few minutes. This part of the day fosters group participation and a feeling of community. What this part of the program is called will vary, depending on the situation and the person leading it. Many centers have an area large enough for thirty to forty children to sit at one time in an actual circle. This is an ideal situation and is often called "circle time". Other centers have limited space for spreading out, but do have a rug area that will accommodate a similar number of children. This is usually called a "group time". The activities presented during this time will largely depend on how much space the children have to move around and also on the make-up of the group. A group with mixed ages is more challenging to control and more difficult to keep interested, but can be very exciting.

Many teachers feel uncomfortable leading a large group. Developing the skills necessary to manage a quality group takes experience, patience, and good observation skills, as well as spontaneity. Teachers often limit themselves to story reading and sharing time. While these are significant parts of an effective group time, they are not by any means all that can be done. Make group or circle time fun, interesting, and diversified.

The keys to a successful group or circle are timing and variety. Timing involves preplanning, using observation to spot restlessness, and the ability to shift gears if an activity is not working well. Variety means expanding the scope of group or circle time to include activities that go up, down, sideways, loud and quiet. Having the children sit in a circle is preferable for many activities such as making a spider web, doing exercises, playing musical instruments, and playing games. For movement activities make sure there is enough room for children to be safe while participating. If your available space limits movement, save these types of activities for times when the children can be divided into smaller groups or can be done outdoors.

Music is an important part of group time. You do not need to play a musical instrument to have fun singing and doing rhythm activities with children. Older children prefer songs that are not the standard preschool type. There are delightful folk songs, silly songs and even modern songs that can be discovered and shared. Other group time activities that are enjoyable are: announcements, simple games, movement activities, sign language or foreign language learning, problem solving, program planning, dramatic activities and theme related projects. For younger children, group time can include: flannel board stories, finger plays and tell-and-draw stories.

Some suggestions for a successful group time are:

1. Vary the length, depending on the age and attention span of the children. Younger children need a shorter time and a smaller group.

2. Start group with an activity that grabs their attention and interest. Then they will be ready to listen or participate.

3. Pace your activities by watching the children's reactions. It is easy to tell when they are bored or restless. Change your tempo accordingly. Do not hesitate to throw out an activity that is not working. Spontaneous activities are perfectly valid.

4. Separate children who have trouble sitting next to each other before starting group time. Another way is to have an adult "ride shotgun," keep a sharp lookout for trouble. By having adults sit down with the children unobtrusively, in strategic locations, many difficulties can be avoided, making it more enjoyable for everyone.

5. Allow a child who cannot comfortably participate to sit or draw at a nearby table, rather than letting him or her disrupt the group.

6. Do not limit group time to indoors or even the school grounds.

7. Alternate different types of activities during group time; i.e. singing, then movement, then a story. Change the lengths of activities also, especially with mixed-age groups.

# RESTING THE KINDERGARTEN CHILDREN

If the kindergarten children come to your program for a half day, then include rest time. Many programs find it quite difficult to have a rest time for the kindergartners because of space and time restrictions. However, the opportunity to have a half-hour rest time, or a one-hour nap time for those who sleep, can be genuinely beneficial. Kindergarten children tend to be very busy during school. This constant activity may be both physically and emotionally stressful for the first few months. Some may cry, wet their pants or have difficulty controlling their behavior. Resting provides their bodies with the much needed chance to relax and calm down. If napping is impossible, at least have the children sit down and rest, or be read to quietly.

*We do have an opportunity for the children to nap at our program. Each child has a cot to rest on and brings a blanket and pillow from home. Out of our thirty kindergartners about twenty usually sleep. The other ten rest and then look at books. When a child who usually sleeps does not for some reason, we can see the difference in his or her behavior as the day goes on.* Napping or resting does help the kindergarten children function better during a very long day. *We do all we can to provide a calm and secure resting time for them.* Towards the end of the school year some of the children out grow a need to take a nap, and they rest rather than sleep.

Here are some hints for a successful rest time:

1. Before rest time, have a group time to calm the children down and also have them use the bathroom.

2. Always have the children use the same cot or mat labeled with their name on it. Have each child bring a sheet, blanket and pillow from home and whatever small item helps him or her be comfortable.

3. Allow children to take books to their cots, but after five minutes or so, have all books put under cots and turn out the lights.

4. Limit napping to one hour; longer periods of time tend to result in children having trouble falling asleep at bedtime.

5. Make a chart of who sleeps and who does not the first week of school; arrange the children around the room accordingly. Strategically place the non-sleepers in places where they do not disturb the sleepers. After a half hour of resting, quiet alternative activities can be made available for non-sleepers.

6. Always place the child's cot or mat in the same place in the room.

7. Rub the backs of children to help them fall asleep; it works wonders! Many children who never take naps will often fall asleep if their backs are rubbed. Back rubbing can be combined with verbal and physical reinforcement for those who are resting quietly. It really does calm down those who are fidgety and allows their bodies to relax. However, some children do not like their backs rubbed and the caregiver must respect the child's wishes. Some programs also have quiet music, adults singing, or taped stories during rest time.

At first, both parents and children may complain. A parent may say; "My child has not slept since he was two!" Make it clear that not all the children are expected to sleep and none are forced. Resting quietly for 20 to 30 minutes is beneficial to all children. Children who complain at first get used to the rest time and many grow to enjoy it. Many children who never used to nap will actually fall asleep.

# THE OLDER CHILDREN

One of the most difficult areas in school-age care is working with the older children. In some programs, fourth through sixth graders are considered "the older children"; *in our program they are third through fifth.* This will vary, depending on the ages served and group sizes. Many older children have been in child care since early childhood and would rather be home on their own. We, as child care professionals, know that it is safer for them to remain in programs, but for the children it can be very frustrating. The needs of the older children are quite different from the kindergartners through second graders. Challenge the older children with activities that meet their interests and developmental levels.

*In our program the third graders have a corner of the large room that is just for them with their own games and books. They often put up signs that state "Third graders, teachers and parents only. All other children KEEP OUT!" The fourth and fifth graders use the school library after school and set it up as a recreational area. They have their own games, hobbies and crafts, equipment, radio and rules. They are free to join the younger children during free play time but the younger children cannot come into their space. This set-up works well with the children in our program.*

Here are some hints for a successful program for older children:

1. Provide a space or area just for them. A separate room is the best solution, but if this is impossible, set up a corner of the room for them. Make this area off-limits for any younger child. Include in this area: age-appropriate games, a rug, a sofa and bean bag chairs or futons, a tape recorder/radio, art supplies, models, etc. Also, equipment such as a caroom board, ping-pong table, air hockey, and a pool table are appropriate. Nerf™ pool or ping-pong sets are great.

2. Many older children have had years of painting and process-oriented art projects. Older children are not as process oriented as younger ones and are ready for kits, models and other challenging projects. They are interested in activities that have a goal to work towards. They also enjoy hands-on messy projects from time to time.

3. Invite the older children to be helpers for the younger children. They can assist during homework time, art time, or snack time. The older children may want to "adopt" a younger child and be their special helper. *This has been very successful in our program.*

4. Allow space away from adults for the older children. Supervise them, but try to keep a proper distance; do not intrude on their personal conversations and space unless it is necessary for safety.

5. Social problem solving and group dynamics are very important for the older group of children. Teachers need to help build a sense of group acceptance and togetherness.

6. Older children must learn to take responsibility for themselves and their actions. They can help set-up their own rules and consequences.

7. Older children especially need ample time to exercise and be outside.

8. Outdoor games should be of their own choosing. Much socializing and modeling goes on at these times. Rules are an important part of the process. Adults should interfere only if rules are unfair or exclude some children.

9. Older children often invent their own games and play them for long periods of time. Encourage this process; it is important for their growth and development.

Beginning hormonal development will result in new found interest in the opposite sex. Children are maturing very early these days and the older group of children may act like adolescents from time to time. There will be sexual talk, embarrassment, modeling of older siblings, and exploration.

Children need to learn the sexual facts correctly. Often the children who are the most sexually verbal are the ones who know the least about the subject. If a group leader plans to discuss sex with the older group of children, a parental permission slip should be signed by each child's parent. This is a legal consideration, especially for programs that function within the public school system. A parent meeting at orientation/enrollment time might be useful and pave the way for uneasy parents. Unfortunately, a child whose parent will not agree to allow them to participate will need to be gently excluded. Remember, even though the teacher may not talk to a particular child, the other children will relay the information.

Discussions about sex are best when they occur naturally, spontaneously, or at the children's request. Keep the discussions honest, simple, and straight forward. If the teacher does not have an answer he or she should say so, and then look it up. There are many good books about this subject.

If you strive to meet the needs of the older group of children, then their time in child care can be more enjoyable for everyone. With a space of their own, the older children will feel they are special and have earned the right to more freedom than the younger ones. The younger children see that they have something to look forward to in your program when they are older.

# AGE GROUPING

School-age children's needs, wants and development are quite different from those of preschool children. While kindergarten-age children still enjoy activities similar to preschoolers' interests, the older children will have nothing to do with "baby stuff". Many caregivers make the mistake of treating children as if they were all the same age. With a range of children from kindergarten to sixth grade and sometimes older, children must be treated according to their developmental and individual needs. Nevertheless, mixed-age grouping, does prove enjoyable for the children. The older children can serve as helpers, friends and role models for the younger ones. However, there should be time when children are age-grouped for specific activities such as certain games, special art activities, science, and other learning or problem solving projects. Vary schedules so that during some times the children are age-grouped, and at other times they can mix freely.

# INTEREST CLUBS

An excellent way to involve the children and staff members is interest clubs. *In our center each staff member writes down a list of activities, hobbies, and areas of expertise which they are interested in teaching to a small group of children. For an hour per week, the children break up into "KIDS' CLUBS". Each child signs up for his or her first three choices, and the staff puts each one into a club. This provides for encouragement for a variety of activities and social groupings. Children participate in their club for four weeks and then sign up for a new one.*

Examples of clubs are:

| | | | |
|---|---|---|---|
| basketball | tumbling | science | wood working |
| music | rug hooking | crocheting | leather crafts |
| sewing | printing | paper folding | candle making |
| tie dying | silk screening | papier-mache | mask making |
| ceramics | drama | dance movement | jazzercise |
| radio show | wrestling | puppet making | computers |
| photography | outdoor games | mural painting | mask making |
| baseball | soccer | paper airplanes | volleyball |
| track | mime | photography | planting and growing |

The ideas are only limited by the staff's capabilities. This provides an excellent way for children to explore areas of interest in depth, learn new skills, and it gives the adults an opportunity to teach children something that they enjoy. The clubs are mixed-aged groups; this allows the older children to interact with and to help the younger ones and vice versa! Interest clubs are wonderful for programs with 40 children or more.

*Our program grew from 30 to 70 children in three years. With the smaller number of children, we were able to do many of the activities in interest clubs as a part of our regular curriculum. As the numbers grew, it became increasingly difficult to do many of these activities. Interest clubs allow large programs to do expensive and more complicated projects with a limited number of children. They have proven to be a very successful part of our curriculum.*

# SUMMER PROGRAMS AND HOLIDAY CARE

The scheduling for all-day programs is quite different from before-and-after-school only. Long blocks of time allow more variety of activities, field trips, and ongoing projects. For all-day care, provide at least two snacks per day, several activity periods, free choice time, much outdoor play and recreation, interesting field trips, and (in the summer) lessons such as karate, swimming and dance. A quiet rest time should be built into the schedule for all children. This can include reading and being read to, doing puzzles, and other quiet activities.

Themes work well for all-day and summer programs. However, many of the children have been in child care since they were very small and have done the standard preschool themes. Try to make the school-age themes as new and engaging as possible. Activities such as snack, dramatic play, art, cooking, field trips, and science can all center around the themes.

Some examples of themes are:

| | | | |
|---|---|---|---|
| ecology | sea shore | bays | space and stars |
| jungles | woodlands | desert | travel and transportation |
| Olympics | countries | camp crafts | international foods |
| other eras | toys | sports | myth and fantasy |
| animals | Black history | fashion | communication |
| energy | technology | magic | electronics |
| dinosaurs | harbors | fads | geographic features |
| rock & roll | pets | collections | weather |
| super heroes | cavemen | the Gold Rush | Disneyland™ |
| reptiles | nature | aeronautics | endangered species |

In summer and holiday programs, emphasize the differences in the program from the school year. When naming a summer session, use a name similar to a summer camp or day camp. This will help change the emphasis and children's attitude. In full day programs emphasize a relaxed, fun atmosphere rather than academics.

An example of our summer program scheduling follows:

| | |
|---|---|
| **7:30-9:00** | Free play |
| **9:00-9:15** | Morning group |
| **9:15-10:30** | Morning activity time (crafts, science, nature, sports) |
| **10:30-10:45** | Snack (AM snack should be light) |
| **10:45-11:45** | Activity time |
| **11:45-12:30** | Clean up and lunch |
| **12:30-1:00** | Outdoor play |
| **1:00-1:15** | Group time (kindergartners calm down for rest) |
| **1:15-1:45** | Resting and quiet activity time (rest from 1:15-2:30) |
| **1:45-3:30** | Activity time (cooking, woodworking,lessons, etc.) |
| **3:30-3:45** | Snack time |
| **3:45-4:00** | Afternoon group (can be broken into small groups)* |
| **4:00-6:00** | Free choice/free play indoors/outdoors |

*One method that works well in summer programs is for each group leader to plan one project a week in a particular interest area. Connect the projects with the themes. Divide the children into age groups (as evenly as possible). Allow each age group a chance to do each teacher's project on a particular day and at a specific time. There are many ways to organize projects for small and larger groups. Test what works best with your staff and children.

For programs that are in a very hot climate, outside time is best in the morning and lots of water play will help beat the heat. For cold weather scheduling, take advantage of the sun. Remember to be flexible with scheduling. Circumstances change and there are no strict time frames. To add excitement to your summer program, schedule in a special event. This can be a game, party, visit from someone to the program, performance by the children, or a contest. *In our summer program we have one special event every two weeks.* The events can be theme related or not.

The following are some ideas for special events:

| | |
|---|---|
| sock hop | lost treasure day |
| carnival | sand castle building contest |
| puppet show | restaurant day |
| backwards day | kite or paper airplane flying contest |
| olympics or relay races | office day (dress like business people) |
| outer space day | detective or mystery day |
| square dancing | build a volcano |
| scavenger hunt day | cartoon dress-up day |
| water play day | soap bubble blowing contest |

# FIELD TRIPS AND SPECIAL PROGRAMS

Field trips are a very important part of school-age programs. Riding public transportation is a new experience for many children and can be very educational. Also many children do not have opportunities to explore their cities, towns, and environments.

Some hints for successful field trips are:

1. When selecting a field trip have a staff member visit the site in advance.

2. It is a good idea to call the place the day before to reconfirm.

3. Be well staffed, include parent volunteers if possible.

4. Each teacher of a group of children should bring along a small first-aid kit, emergency releases, tissues and/or wet wipes.

5. Dress the children in a school t-shirt (red or yellow are good colors to see in a crowd), or other identifying article of clothing such as a scarf or a baseball cap. Each child should bring a jacket or sweater.

6. Have children bring lunches in paper bags stowed inside their back packs; (no glass containers.)

7. Make sure the children know ahead of time the field trip rules, are aware of where and why they are going, and what mode of transportation is being used.

8. When walking in small groups (4-10), the adult should walk in the middle of the group (if there is only one adult). For larger groups or situations were there are two or more adults, have one adult lead the group, one adult in the middle and one adult at the end of the line.

9. Children should never cross the street alone and should stay within the crosswalks. For crowded intersections, have one adult stand in the middle of the street to stop traffic if necessary.

10. Encourage the children to write thank you notes when appropriate.

Some suggestions for field trips are visits to the following:

| | | | |
|---|---|---|---|
| museums | the zoo | parks | Botanical Gardens |
| a bowling alley | hospitals | boat rides | children's movie |
| baseball games | picnics | bakery | city or neighborhood walks |
| swimming pools | pet shops | fishing | TV or radio stations |
| skating rink | a play | the circus | the mountains |
| a puppet show | the beach | a farm | factories/plants |
| horseback riding | the airport | the country | the arboretum |
| wildlife preserves | a train ride | libraries | miniature golf |
| recreation centers | restaurants | shows | a ferry boat ride |

(Whatever is interesting and accessible in your area.)

Some areas do not have good public transportation systems available. If it is too difficult to manage many field trips, then in-house field trips or special events can be substituted, or used to enrich program themes. Many museums have programs that come to schools. For information and vehicle tours, invite public service people such as police, fire and paramedics to visit your center. The local animal pound worker, park and recreation forest ranger, zoo staff person, or veterinarian may bring in animals. Arrange for a mime troop, a clown, folk singers or a story teller to come and perform. Parents, business persons, and others such as grandparents, aunts, uncles, friends, and neighbors may also volunteer to talk about their professions. Also invite hobbyists, retired persons that have special interests, farmers, professional athletes and professional organizations to speak. These people help to diversify the children's experiences and give them something out of the ordinary to look forward to while in full-day programs.

Walking trips to parks, historical or local sites, and trails can be valuable when transportation is not possible.

There are several things to remember for walking trips:

1. Make sure the distance is manageable for the age group going.
2. Find a place to rest along the way before starting out.
3. Carry water and paper cups, and easy snack for energy.
4. Always have at least two adults present.
5. Prepare ahead for weather, especially during fall and spring.
6. Advise children and staff to wear walking shoes.

Using parents' cars for field trips raises questions about insurance coverage. Ask your insurance agent to research the best method for making field trips possible. Try asking the local Rotary Club, Elks Club or other organizations to donate a van and keep it serviced. Do what you can to GET OUT with your children!

# PARENT/TEACHER COMMUNICATION

Parents of kindergarten-age children need special consideration. Even if the child has attended preschool, both parent and child are experiencing a new process of letting go and are in the middle of an important transition. Kindergarten is often very different from preschool or child care and the behaviors and expectations frequently are more demanding for the children. They are entering an academic world and their parents are entering a new relationship with them. For some the transition is smooth; for others it is a rough one. Patience and calm support are beneficial for them during this year.

However, parents' attachment to children is not related to age; they all have similar concerns. Working parents have special stresses, the hardest of which is the lack of time and energy for their children, and the guilt that often results. Parents with financial problems, coupled with family stress are especially in need of extra patience from child care staff. For some working parents their only social life is the chats they have at the child care center.

Parents have a great investment in their children and most identify strongly with their success and failures. Competent parents may have a child with behavior problems for reasons other than their parenting skills. Assistance may be necessary to put their parenting in perspective.

Talking to parents is often difficult. Most interactions between parents and staff are brief and hurried. Working parents often do not have a great deal of time to communicate with staff members. They are busy, tired and sometimes impatient. Many parents arrive near closing time; the staff members are also tired and impatient to go home. This is a sensitive time of the day and requires gentle handling. It falls on the staff to be professional during these moments. Some form of communication is essential when parents come to pick up their children. This can be eye contact and a smile, a tactful inquiry, or help getting the child ready to leave.

A child who is in the middle of a project or a game may not want to leave. Teachers can help by reminding the child that the parent wants to leave right away and that they can, in most cases, continue to work on their project the next day. Often this reassurance means the difference between a war of wills and peaceful coexisting. A parent in a hurry would rather not have to wait for a clean-up. However, it is important that the child does clean-up before leaving, so that the child learns to take responsibility for his or her actions. The caregiver may have to remind the parent of its importance. A few moments of transition time before going home is often necessary. If parents allow five to ten minutes for children to finish up, the results are often far more relaxed than always rushing children out the door. Caregivers can use these five minutes to assist the children, talk to the parents, or both.

Perhaps the hardest thing about parent/staff communication is knowing how to describe a child's difficulties without making the parent feel it is their fault, or that they are in some way a "bad" parent. Parents are sensitive about their roles as working parents. They may resent the relationships that teachers develop with their children, considering how little time during the week they have to spend with them. Parents depend on child care and, as a result, often have mixed feelings about it. They may resent a teacher who does not have children of his or her own because they feel that the teacher lacks the day-to-day home life aspect of child development.

When saying something negative about a child to a parent, try to approach it in a positive manner. For example, instead of saying "Alex has been hitting other children" you might say, "Alex is having trouble controlling his temper. We are working together on a solution to the problem and we would like your help." Constructive support and comments are often necessary. Parents do appreciate a teacher's observations and suggestions.

There will inevitably be a parent or a child that a caregiver does not particularly like. Some people feel that they must like all children in the program and then experience great conflict and guilt when personalities clash. Remember, everyone is human. Professionally, even if an adult does not like a child, he or she must always have the child's best interests in mind.

In cases when a staff member does not get along well with a parent he may choose to:

- share something interesting the child did
- ask how the parent's day was
- tell what kind of day the child had
- or let someone else say hello if that is easier.

Children and families have a variety of needs and your program may not be the solution for every family. When a child's individual problems are so severe that they disrupt the balance and flow of the entire program, it is time to consider other possibilities. We cannot be everything to every child and family. This is a hard concept to grasp but we must look at the good of the program as a whole. It is very difficult to ask a family to remove their child from a program, but it may be the best solution. In this case, help the family to locate another program, counselling, or other assistance.

Some suggestions for communicating with parents are:

1. Learn the parents' names and ask them for information about their lifestyle but be sensitive to and respect their privacy.

2. Be creative; say something positive about their child whenever possible.

3. Keep parental confidences private.

4. Discuss only essential details of incidents, avoid naming other children whenever possible.

5. Timing is important; it takes practice and patience to learn that some things can wait.

6. When writing a newsletter or handbook, include a section on going home and transition times.

7. Remember, a sense of humor is essential when working with parents and their children.

# CONFLICT RESOLUTION

Conflict resolution is the process of mediating between children who are not getting along in a way that helps them learn to think situations through for themselves. Teachers can intervene and time children out, but often that only delays the problem, or leaves it unresolved for the children. Children need help learning creative ways to deal with conflict situations, and learning to decide which idea is the most constructive at the time.

School-age children fall into one of two stages generally. They are either in the "scratch my back and I'll scratch yours" stage or the "rules are rules, and that's that" stage. Younger children are usually willing to compromise if they get something out of it in return. But older children are more often set on "the way it is supposed to be for everyone", and inconsistency is intolerable for them. Children can be helped through these stages by use of conflict resolution strategies.

There are five stages on which to focus during conflict resolution:

1. Stop the conflict. Calm the children down. Separate them if necessary. If there has been physical injury, tend to the hurt first. When the children are calmer, go on. Sit between them if they are still very angry.

2. Define the specific problem. This means to listen carefully to all the children involved in what happened. Concentrate on identifying the specific problem. "She's mean to me," is not specific enough. Make sure the children elaborate. "I had it first and she took it." or "She says I have to do her homework or she won't be my friend." Try to assess the main conflict, without judging or criticizing or finding out who "started it". "I see, you both want to play with the pogo ball."

3. Have the children come up with ideas about how to change the situation, how to fix it, or what they could have done differently. Get lots of ideas from all the children involved. Do not stop when one idea sounds good; collect a few first. "What else?" is a handy tool. It is very hard sometimes, but be careful not to suggest ideas yourself. Children will often have angry ideas first. Go on until they are past that, without judging their ideas. "I could hit her." "Yes, you could, what else?"

4. When there are several ideas available, then it is time to evaluate them. Repeat their ideas back to them without critical comment and ask them what would happen next in each case. "You said you could hit her. What would happen then?" "What will happen if you do not do your homework?" Go through all the ideas and let the children tell you what the consequences of their suggestions might be. They may say, "She'd hit me back." Or "I'd get a time out."

5. Then they need to decide on the solution that sounds best and plan how to follow it through.

This process works. It can be an effective teaching and learning tool. However, it can also lead to the over-verbalization and wordiness trap. Avoid long speeches and keep the resolution time as brief as possible. Children are often anxious to keep moving. Adults are sometimes slower to recognize their need to put an incident behind them and continue playing.

The generation of ideas and the evaluation process are important parts of what conflict resolution and problem solving are all about. Encourage children's thinking and analyzing skills whenever possible.

# PROJECTS

## Public Schools

The focus in most public schools for many years has been getting back to the "basics". Academics are stressed. One of the best aspects of working with children after school is being able to supplement what is lacking in the classroom, and provide a balance for the children served. Care providers should visit the children's classrooms to observe what is emphasized and plan their activities accordingly, to broaden, enrich and supplement.

Children generally receive very little hands on exposure to art, problem solving and science. To many teachers, art means a specific lesson or preconceived purpose; the results come out looking the same. Art projects in elementary schools tend to be product-oriented rather than process. Very few teachers, in grades higher than kindergarten, put out an easel and encourage free expression or allow the children to just "mess around" with paint. An easel is a great gift to some children. Hands-on and experimental type science projects are often missing from many school curricula. The projects in this book were chosen with these factors in mind.

## Planning And Project Set-Up

During the planning process of a particular project there are many components to keep in mind. The most important are the ages, interests and abilities of the children. Projects should be planned well in advance to allow for special materials to be purchased. Science projects and experiments with a specific goal should be tested out in advance to insure the teacher knows what to expect. Make children a part of the planning process. Ask children what projects interest and excite them and let them know that their ideas and suggestions are important. Remember that when planning a project it is critical to allocate enough time for the children to explore the medium. All creative approaches are acceptable.

Set-up is critical when presenting a project. Children can help set-up the materials. *In our program the children enjoy mixing paints, putting newspaper on the art table, making dough or clay and cutting out materials for projects.* Make sure that all the materials are available and in large enough quantities for the majority of children doing the activity. If the project is messy, covering the table with newspaper, butcher paper or plastic will prevent a long clean-up. If the materials are presented in an attractive way, the children will be more likely to give the project a try. Make sure there is plenty of room for all the materials needed or set some aside for later use.

Give each child his or her own materials, or easy access to shared materials. If a table cannot accommodate all the children choosing to do the project, start a waiting list and have the children call each other when a space becomes available. When doing a project, observe what seems to work well and what does not and use this information for future planning.

## Projects and Activities With Food

There are activities and projects in this book that include the use of food. This is admittedly a controversial practice, because there is so much hunger in the world. For many children, items like rice and beans are staples of their daily diet. It is difficult for them to understand why this food is being used in a non-nutritive fashion. Be sensitive to this problem. We have included these projects because even though they are controversial, they still have educational and hands-on value. We provide a wide variety of activities, including alternatives to the use of food, whenever possible. Develop your own philosophy regarding the use of food, and use discretion.

## Open-Ended Projects

During after school child care there are long periods of time which children can use for arts, crafts, and other projects. Present children with an opportunity to do *open-ended* projects. In an *open-ended* or *process-oriented* project, the outcome is not important, rather the emphasis is the process the child goes through in creating the project. *Open-ended* means that there is no expectation for a final result, and that a finished product can vary depending on the child's interests, ideas and skills.

The process of using the materials and exploring the possibilities of each medium is the main focus of *open-ended* activities. There are no wrong or right ways to create them. It is the difference between having twenty items that come out looking exactly the same or having each item reflect the individual child's prospective. In a *closed-ended* or *product-oriented project*, the outcome is the most important result. These projects are known as "parent pleasers." They have certain expected outcomes and teachers help the children achieve these. Individuality and creativity aside, children's small motor skills are often not well developed and it is frustrating for them to be asked to try to copy a teacher-made model, especially if it is an intricate or detailed activity.

Having an area where children can choose projects for themselves gives them a chance to explore and develop their creative skills. Support and encourage children but never do the project for them. They have an endless ability to create new and imaginative things out of any given material. Allow children to stretch and challenge their skills through their own creativity. Open-ended projects can include drama, arts and crafts, and science and nature exploration.

## Kits and Finished Products

As children grow and mature and have many experiences creating open-ended projects, they become ready for kits and finished products. Usually children in third grade and older enjoy doing kits such as basket weaving, string art, leather crafts, or beading. There should also be a chance for the children to further their drawing skills. Lessons in perspective and tips for drawing "correctly" are useful at this age when the need is presented. A balance between kits and open-ended art projects is advisable. The process is still the most valuable aspect, but the product begins to take on its own importance. Finished products in science are exciting, but the process of inquiry is what should be the prime focus. Allow time and offer opportunities to use the material more than one way!

## Examples

Examples are not usually necessary. Many teachers do not want a preconceived end product, but rather, desire children to be able to create their own outcome to particular projects. However, there are times when a planned project is set on the art table, and, without an example, it would be very difficult for the children to envision what they can achieve with the materials. In these cases, after showing an example, put it out of sight to allow individual variation and creativity. Examples should always look like a child has created them and several diverse examples are even better. When the examples look like they were created by an adult, children may feel frustrated that their work is "not as good" as the adult. Save pieces of children's work to use as examples for the future. After the project is completed, evaluate whether the model was necessary for future presentation.

## Unsuccessful Projects

It is very important for child care workers to understand that not every project is going to be a success! What works well with one group of children can be a disaster with another. Even the most carefully planned project may not work out as anticipated. If a project is not successful for one reason or another, it is not the end of the world. Even the most experienced teacher has a project fail from time to time. The most important thing is that the teacher evaluate the project to try to determine why the project failed.

In other words, to learn from their mistakes. In many cases the adult leader will discover that the failure was due to other factors out of the adult's control. *We have found in our center that children tend to react to many outside elements. These can include the weather and the wind, testing going on in the school, or the time of the year (near a holiday or a vacation raises activity levels).* Keeping this in mind can alleviate teachers' feelings of frustration and stress that go along with unsuccessful projects.

The children are not to blame for an unsuccessful project. It is our professional responsibility to support the children when projects are not successful. They need reassurance that the goof-up was not their fault and that their feelings of frustration and anger are acceptable. When the failure is due to something that can be altered in the set-up or the process, make a note of it and try again. Experiment with changing some of the materials or tools, the procedure, timing, location, or the age group of the children. During a project, it is sometimes easy to spot what is going wrong. Do not hesitate to correct it right away.

Science projects often go awry due to timing, the group make-up, or unfamiliarity with either the process or the materials. Trying out a project ahead of time will help prevent (but not necessarily eliminate) the failure syndrome when a specific result is desired. Other times, as long as a teacher is familiar with the use of materials, there is no failure possible. The process of exploring provides its own success, no matter what the consequences are.

Real life problem solving — a ball that needs air

# PROBLEM SOLVING

Problem solving is the process which teaches children how to find answers to situations when the means to the solution is not necessarily obvious. It is "what to do when you don't know what to do." Teaching problem solving involves teaching children strategies for figuring out different ways to reach a conclusion.

Problem solving is a very important part of learning for children, and has recently been considered a major component to be developed and utilized in the California State school curriculum. Problem solving can be used in conjunction with all subjects including math, reading, language arts, social studies, arts, and social skill development. Many problem solving games and activities take only a few minutes to plan and to execute, and are usually fun as well as challenging.

It is important in teaching problem solving to state the technique you want children to learn during the game or activity, but not before they have had time to find it for themselves. The keys to problem solving, whatever the subject, are time and patience. You are teaching a thinking process; that means that some children will pick it up very quickly, and others will need repeated activities and more exposure to the process. It is essential that these games be fun for the children and do not appear to be work or "lessons".

Problem solving skills are a part of daily life for all adults. It is important that children have access to the techniques that will make it possible for them to function as completely as possible in all areas of their interests and needs. Many schools and teachers do not yet use problem solving concepts in their teaching process. This is a valuable area for after school providers to explore and expand. It can be exciting to see the interest and enthusiasm generated by these activities, and to watch the growth of skills and techniques in children.

## STEPS IN PROBLEM SOLVING:

**1.** Gather information (in game situations the teacher provides this.)

**2.** State the problem clearly. Define it.

**3.** Generate ideas to solve the problem.

**4.** Evaluate the answers and the process.

# PROBLEM SOLVING STRATEGIES TO TEACH CHILDREN

This is a list of the strategies used to solve problems. Children should to be taught these methods so they can rely on them. When one does not work, they need to be able to try another. This list is based on the California State framework for Problem Solving. Each of these strategies can be applied to almost any problem area. They are all valuable to children and adults. See which ones are techniques that you use to solve your own problems.

**1.** Look for patterns

**2.** Guess and check

**3.** Write equations - (if... = ....,then.....)

**4.** Logical reasoning

**5.** Working backwards

**6.** Draw pictures of the problem or situation

**7.** List information

**8.** Make tables or graphs

**9.** Act out or use hands-on equipment

**10.** Simplify the problem by breaking into smaller parts first

## PICO, FERMI, BAGELS

*PURPOSE:* A problem solving game that teaches place value, and works something like the game Master Mind™.

*MATERIALS:* Chalk and chalk board, or large paper and marking pen placed on a wall for visibility.

*GRADES:* 2 - 6

*PROCEDURE:*

1. Have children sit in group in front of the writing surface.

2. Explain that you are going to play a game with them that involves two digit numbers (this can be expanded to three or four later). You are writing down a number between 10-99 where they cannot see it. They have to guess what it is in the fewest number of guesses possible.

3. As they guess a number, you write it on the grid on the number side and then give them their clues on the other side.

4. The clues are: PICO-means there is one number right but it is in the wrong place. FERMI-means there is one number right and it is in the right place. BAGELS-means that there are no numbers right at all in their guess. (Explain to them that BAGELS is a very good clue to get and show them why the first few times). Give double clues if two numbers are correct but in the wrong place, i.e. pico, pico.

5. The first few times this is played it is a good idea to walk the group through the process of guessing by having the numbers 0-9 on the board also. Help them see the process of elimination by actually erasing or crossing out the numbers that are not usable after each guess. Circle those numbers that may be possible answers.

6. Start with unlimited number of guesses. When they have grasped the idea, limit them to 10 guesses.

*COMMENTS:*

Children learn a strategy of elimination and of logical reasoning.

This game is a lot of fun. Be sure to validate each child's guess somehow, such as: "good guess" or "OK, that guess will help eliminate these numbers."

## HALF LOGIC OR HIGHER/LOWER

*PURPOSE:* A very good beginning number game that teaches the strategy of halving number columns, and the concept of elimination.

*MATERIALS:* Large paper and pen or chalk board and chalk.

*GRADES:* 1 - 5

*PROCEDURE:*

1. List the numbers 1-25 on the paper or board in a column. Increase the list as the children gain confidence.

2. Have children sit in front of the writing surface.

3. Tell them that this is a guessing game. You are hiding a number between 1-25 and they have to figure it out by asking questions.

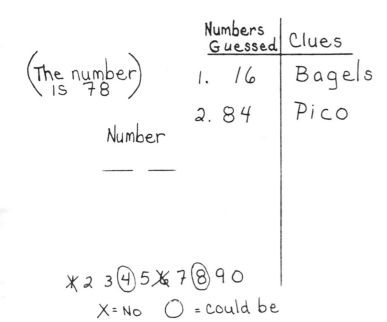

(The number is 78)

Number

| Numbers Guessed | Clues |
|---|---|
| 1. 16 | Bagels |
| 2. 84 | Pico |

___  ___

X 2 3 ④ 5 X 7 ⑧ 9 0

X = No    ◯ = could be

4. They cannot guess specific numbers, they must ask if the hidden number is higher or lower; for example is it higher than 15?. The teacher can only answer yes or no. (Asking if a number is between two others gets tricky; save that for later).

5. The teacher can also say "that was a good question," because there is a strategy to guessing that you want them to figure out.

6. Play the game without telling them what the strategy is for a while. Then, ask them if they have noticed it.

7. When a child guesses in a way that eliminates a large block of numbers, call it to the group's attention and ask them why it was a good question.

8. The strategy this game is looking for is cutting the column in half each time a question is asked, reducing the quantity of numbers to be considered each time.

9. After the group has tried this several times, tell them that now it is a contest between the teacher and them. If they guess the number in less than ten questions, they get a point; if not, then the teacher gets a point. Keep score, and have fun! As they get more adept at this, reduce the number of allowable guesses for increased challenge.

## COMMENTS:

A group that has developed this strategy will be able to get a number in less than 5-6 questions. It becomes a real exciting challenge to "beat the teacher," no matter how many numbers are used.

## BUILDING A BETTER BATHTUB

*PURPOSE:* To warm up a group, provide inclusion for all children, demonstrate the fun and power of brainstorming as a technique for solving problems. Good for grades K - 8.

*MATERIALS:* Large piece of paper and marking pen for each team.

*GRADES:* K - 8

*PROCEDURE:*

1. Break group into teams of four. (Or fewer if your group is small).

2. Provide each team with large paper and a marking pen.

3. Tell them that each team is going to design a better bathtub.

4. They need to select one member of each team to write down the ideas.

5. They are to discuss what would work by taking turns around their table and writing every idea down as quickly as possible, without comment or judgment. Encourage ideas that are offbeat and unique. They have five minutes for this part.

6. Stop the teams after 5 minutes.

7. Next they are to discuss the ideas individually, clarify any confusing ones, allow each person to further explain their idea. This part should take 10 minutes. Allow every team member a turn in sequence.

8. Stop the teams again and tell them that they will now vote on the ideas they want to keep in their bathtub. They will read each idea and vote it up or down. Majority vote wins. Items not making it are crossed out. This should take another 5 minutes.

9. Bring the group back together to present their finished ideas for a better bathtub.

10. Discuss the whole process. How did they feel doing it? Were some of the ideas silly? Was it hard not to comment or criticize ideas? Was it fun?

11. This can be done with any type of machine.

## COMMENTS:

This activity was adapted from Tribes, please see the Resource Section for more information

## BUMPER STICKER

*PURPOSE:* To encourage listening skills; to include every child.

*MATERIALS:* Long thin paper, about 4" x 10", marking pens or crayons.

PROCEDURE:

1. Sit children at tables and provide them each with paper and writing tools.

2. They are to make a bumper sticker of their own choice out of the paper. Give them about 10-15 minutes.

3. Have each child share his or her bumper sticker with the class. Take volunteers at first.

4. Put the papers up where they can be seen by every one and give time to read them all.

5. Go around the group and ask each person to tell which ones they might actually use, which ones surprised them, which ones they like best. Discuss the purpose that each bumper sticker seems to express such as a point of view, advertisement, or communication.

COMMENTS:

This activity adds a different perspective to the group. It is fun and imaginative, and often surprising.

## LOGIC GRIDS

These are language oriented games that involve the use of a grid to plot given information. They are designed to enhance logical reasoning skills. Children love these problems and develop increasing skill with them as the problems contain more information and variables. The book Logic Anyone? (see the Resource Section) contains a good selection of these grid problems. Once you have the idea of how they work, you and the children can design your own with subjects and information that are relevant to your school or neighborhoods. The children can give their problems to the others to solve.

*Example:* Nancy, Jerry, Jan, and Rob are all artists. One of them uses only felt pens, one uses only water colors, one uses only crayons, and one uses only black pencils. Find out what each person uses with these clues:

1. Jan loves to use bright colors, but does not like felt pens.

2. Rob and Jan never have paint on their hands, but their friend does.

3. Nancy takes very good care of her brushes.

4. Jerry thinks black pencils are boring.

Children use the grid to plot the information and to see the solution more easily. X out the non possible choices. There are lots of these types of problems available, and inventing their own is quite a challenge for children.

## BRAIN TEASERS

These are word problems that contain a twist that makes figuring out the answer a bit tricky. There are several sources for these problems, including some textbooks. These are fun to do as a whole group, or in teams to see which can figure it out first.

| | felt pens | water colors | crayons | black pencils |
|---|---|---|---|---|
| Nancy | | | | |
| Jerry | | | | |
| Jan | | | | |
| Rob | | | | |

Logic Grid

*Sample:* Two mothers and two daughters each won a prize at the fair in the baseball throw booth. These were the last three prizes given away at that booth that day. How is that possible? Answer: There was a grandmother, mother, and daughter.

Start with the simpler ones and work the children into the more complex. Some teachers present these, but usually as homework or as an aside, so some of the older children may have experienced some of the questions. Let those children be monitors, or search for new ones to present.

## SPONTANEOUS PROBLEMS

The idea of the spontaneous problem is to allow the children to use their imagination freely to create unusual solutions in a given time limit. This encourages flexibility and also team work. The ideas presented are from the <u>Odyssey of the Mind</u> training packet. Odyssey of the Mind is a competition of problem solving skills for children of all ages. Regional and then national contests are held each year, with specific problems preplanned, and some spontaneous at the time of the competition. See the Resource Section for more information.

### Spontaneous Problem #1
### A LONG PAPER

*MATERIALS:* One piece 5 1/2" X 8 1/2" paper, scissors, and small piece of tape for each child.

*GRADES:* 3 - 5

*PROCEDURE:*

1. Time limit: 30 minutes.

2. Tell students: You have a piece of paper 5 1/2" X 8 1/2", scissors, and a small piece of tape. You are to cut the paper any way you want, then tape one edge to the floor. You will extend the paper as far as it will reach without breaking. All students will extend their paper at the same time. They must complete the cutting before any exten-

sion takes place. If the paper breaks, where it broke is the distance scored.

*COMMENTS:*

This activity stirs up a lot of interest, discussion and creative thinking, as well as some real friendly competition.

### Spontaneous Problem #2
### SOAP

*MATERIALS:* None

*GRADES:* 2 - 5

*PROCEDURE:*

1. Time Limit — one minute to think, two minutes to respond for each team.

2. Tell children — They have a million bars of soap. What unusual things can they do with them? They get one point for every response, three for those that are interesting or creative.

3. Divide them into teams of four. The points are given to the teams.

4. Teams must not discuss ahead of time.

5. Teams answer in sequence, one answer per teammate, and may not skip turns or repeat or pass.

6. If a team member is stuck, the whole team is stuck.

7. Once time is started, it will not be stopped.

8. The opinion of the judge is subjective and final.

*COMMENTS:*

Quick thinking games like this one are fun, fast and very exhilarating for many children. As they get used to doing this type of problem they begin to understand the pace and the criteria. Team spirit develops with encouragement and discussion afterwards. Was it hard? Did you get frustrated? What did you like about it? Invent questions for them, and let them invent questions for each other.

# SOCIAL PROBLEM SOLVING

Social problem solving involves building the respect and dignity of each person in the group. Group activities that foster sharing, communication, and support are a vital part of the role of the after school situation. Children need to feel that they are important and that their ideas and opinions have value. They also need to develop awareness of the ideas and experiences of others. The Tribes training system (see the Resource Section) offers a method for presenting group sharing games and the Tribes manual is an excellent source of ideas and activities that introduce people to each other and allow them to learn, share, and accept differences. These methods can be very helpful in combating the pressure of peer conformity and the clique tendencies of older children. These concepts and games can also be extended into other areas of family life and after school programs.

There are other books listed in the Resource Section that have group communication games that enhance children's ability to decide and speak for themselves, while still acknowledging the individuality of their friends.

## SOCIAL PROBLEM SOLVING ACTIVITIES

In all activities of this nature there are several rules that need to be taught and adhered to by everyone, including the teacher.

**1.** The right to pass — anyone may choose not to talk.

**2.** No put downs — any idea is worth discussion.

**3.** Good listening — courtesy and attention when another talks.

**4.** Confidentiality — what is said is not discussed out of group.

## THUMBS UP/DOWN

*PURPOSE:* This game helps children to develop decision making skills, express their opinions visibly, and be aware of different opinions. It can help focus on the strength of peer pressure.

*MATERIALS:* A list of age-appropriate questions or statements. (Teacher makes these up. Example: "Hot dogs taste better than hamburgers.")

*GRADES:* K - 6

*PROCEDURE:*

1. Sit whole group in a circle on chairs

2. Explain the rules

    a. The teacher will make a statement, the children will indicate if they agree with it or not.

    b. If they strongly agree they are to clap and cheer loudly

    c. If they agree they are to raise thumbs up

    d. If they disagree they give thumbs down

    e. If they strongly disagree they are to boo, hiss, and stamp

    f. If they have no opinion they are to fold their arms and say nothing at all.

3. When you have asked all questions, it is time to discuss the process:

    a. Was it hard to do? Allow each child to talk by going around the circle quickly.

    b. Did their friends vote differently?

    c. Did they find themselves changing their votes?

    d. What did they feel while doing this game?

4. Go around the circle again and have every child state something that they liked or did not like about the game.

*COMMENTS:*

This game lets children see how easily they are swayed by a group. It works as a great confidence builder especially for children who are reluctant to vocalize their opinions due to peer pressure. Make sure the questions are non-threatening, and not likely to change any current rules in the program.

##  I LIKE MY NEIGHBOR

*PURPOSE:* To include every child, promote awareness of similarities and differences.

*MATERIALS:* Enough chairs or carpet squares for each child.

*GRADES:* K - 6

*PROCEDURE:*

1. Sit children in circle on chairs facing inward.

2. The teacher starts, so there is one chair too few.

3. Explain the rules:

a. The person with no chair will say, "I like my neighbors, especially those with _____ (brown hair, tennis shoes, etc.)"

b. When the person in the middle says something that the children have, they are to get up quickly and move to another chair.

c. The children must get up, and may not sit in their own chair again, and may not stay in the middle on purpose.

d. One person is left with no chair again. It is their turn to call something out.

e. There is no pushing, running, sliding, or sitting on another child.

*COMMENTS:*

This is a very noisy and active game. It allows all of the children all to feel like part of the group and to experience the excitement.

## SPIDER WEB

*PURPOSE:* Developing verbal, sharing, and listening skills.

*MATERIALS:* Large ball of yarn

*GRADES:* K - 6

*PROCEDURE:*

1. Seat group in a circle.

2. Ask any one question appropriate for your group, i.e. What is your favorite thing about autumn? What was the best, or worse, thing that happened to you this weekend?.

3. Teacher starts. Hold the yarn ball and give your answer. Wrap the end of the yarn around your fingers or wrist and toss the ball across the circle from you. Name the person you are tossing it to.

4. The person who gets the ball answers the question, wraps the yarn around their wrist or hand, and tosses it across again, naming who they are throwing it to.

5. This process continues until everyone in the group has had a turn to talk and has the yarn wrapped. The last person should throw the yarn ball back to the teacher who started it, completing the web.

6. Look at the web of communication you have made and discuss it. Talk about how it would be different if it was done again. Look under it, over it, and even through it.

7. Putting it away can be done two ways:

   a. Lay the web down and dismiss the children, you roll it up.

   b. If you have time, reverse the procedure, and see if they can remember what the person who threw the ball to them said.

*COMMENTS:*

This activity lets children see clearly how much they are a part of the group, and how group communication changes and relates. This activity was adapted from Tribes, please see the Resource Section for more information.

## GRAFFITI

*PURPOSE:* To encourage sharing feelings and provide exposure to the wide range of values in any given group.

*MATERIALS:* A large sheet of paper for each group, large marking pens.

*GRADES:* 2 - 6

*PROCEDURE:*

1. Divide children into groups of four.

2. Give each group one piece of large paper with one of the following headings:

*Pet Peeves …*
*Favorite Moments …*
*Things That Scare Me …*
*Things That Make Me Happy…*
*Things That Make Me Curious…*

3. Each team will spend 3 minutes on the first paper. They may write any way they want, wherever they choose. After 3 minutes they must stop writing. Pass each paper to a different group. Allow 3 minutes again. Repeat this process until every team has had each of the papers.

4. Step four can be done either of two ways, depending on the size of your whole group. Either: 1. Give each team one sheet and allow them 10 minutes to discuss trends. Then each team will present what they found to the whole group. Or: 2. Put the graffiti papers up and have the whole group spend a few minutes looking at them, then spend 10 minutes discussing what they see, i.e. similarities, differences, and other comparisons between group answers.

*COMMENTS:*

This activity promotes a lot of comments and laughter. Be prepared for some unusual and diverse "graffiti" to discuss.

---

**Things That Make Me Happy:**

- summer vacation
- going to the movies
- roller skating
- ice cream
- reading a good book

---

# ROUGH AND TUMBLE PLAY

Teachers in day care are primarily female, and often sensitive and caring people. Because of this they are usually very quick to spot rough play and to redirect it to a more focused or quieter activity. There is research and experimentation recently that is beginning to question the value of halting all rough play. Most, though by no means all, of the children engaging in roughhousing type of play are boys. They jump on each other, wrestle, play hit, push, chase, yell and generally raise the energy level in any school yard or room. While this may not be conducive to a calm program, it probably should be encouraged in a structured way that allows room and time for the children to channel this energy in safe ways.

There are obvious differences between the body language of those children who are engaged in play fighting and those who are seriously angry. A seriously angry child may have closed fists, an angry expression on his or her face and may use unacceptable language. Whereas children participating in rough and tumble play tend to laugh, have open fists, have friendly facial expressions, and use bantering words. Pellegrini and Perlmutter found in their research article in the January 1988 issue of Young Children that boys who engaged successfully in rough and tumble had better developed social skills and were more liked by their peers in general. They found that those who did not function well in play fight situations, or in games with rules and strategies, more often could not relate to their peers without becoming angry, were less socially skilled, and less liked. This research could be an important beginning to finding ways to help children with poor social coping skills. Rough and tumble play can teach them to relate better with peers and enjoy playground activities more. The skills they learn in normal, supervised, rough and tumble activities can be applied to other types of social situations.

While there are no firm conclusions yet, the research shows that roughhousing is a very normal way for many children to relate to each other. Fathers play with their children generally with more toss and bounce than do mothers. It is a form of demonstrating affection and love. Children whose parents show affection in these ways learn that it is safe to tell a friend you like them by pushing, jumping on, and wrestling with them. Instead of negating their spontaneous show of friendship, it would be healthier to allow them to express that energy and affection in organized activities.

Girls will benefit from this type of activity also. Many girls have few opportunities to learn the rules of team sports, to assert themselves, or to engage in assertive play. These girls are often timid first, but establish their courage with practice. While they develop a new type of self confidence, they are also developing a new awareness of themselves. They look forward to the wrestling time and begin to want to go against the boys. For aggressive girls, this controlled environment is an acceptable outlet for otherwise discouraged behavior. *The girls in our program are some of the most interested participants when we wrestle.*

# SOME SUGGESTIONS FOR SAFE ROUGHHOUSING:

**1.** Set a time limit for the whole activity, half an hour is good.

**2.** Define the space.

**3.** Use mats, carpets, or other soft surfaces.

**4.** Have children remove shoes and belts, and other accessories.

**5.** Supervise adequately, two teachers is best.

**6.** If there is an injury, stop, attend to the child, then continue. Injuries are usually heads and egos.

**7.** Remind children that this is for fun only; not to hurt, get even, or compete.

**8.** Watch body language. If a child gets upset, have them stop and wait until they are calm again.

**9.** Children not following directions must leave the area for the rest of the activity time. **Give only one warning.** This is important.

**10.** No pulling clothes, biting, kicking, pinching, choking, punching or other injurious action. With attention to these rules, this type of activity will NOT degenerate into fighting.


Rick Porter, Executive Director of Rainbow River Child Care Center has written articles, appeared on television shows, and has been traveling around the United States giving workshops that have a good range of ideas for constructively channeling this type of energy in after-school programs. He now has a video for sale for educational professionals called "Roughhousing — A Guide to Safe and Fun Physical Play for Children," (available through After School, 1401 John Street, Manhattan Beach, California, 90266). Some of the activities below come from his experiences. Many roughhousing ideas can be taken from children's own natural activities in home environments with friends and siblings. These "games" can be altered and supervised in such a way that makes them harmless and successful in the day care situation.

## WRESTLING

*MATERIALS:* A large mat or two small ones and enough space for the safety of the onlookers, a watch with a second hand, a whistle (optional).

*GRADES:* K-6

*PROCEDURE:*

1. Explain the rules.

   a. Wrestle only with an adult at the mat.

   b. Open fists at all times.

   c. No kicking, biting, hair pulling, pinching, choke holds or head locks, high body slams, or karate chops. (Use your judgment)

   d. Wrestlers must stay on the mat, spectators must stay off.

   e. No activity starts until the whistle blows or a signal is given and it stops immediately when it repeats.

   f. Matches last 60-120 seconds depending on the age of the children.

   g. If a child gets upset or injured, they should say so.

   h. Matches need to be even in terms of size at first. Girls will not necessarily always wrestle other girls.

2. Spectators sit on the sidelines AND MUST STAY THERE. Spectators who wrestle out of turn are removed from the area entirely. Cheering is for both participants.

3. The teacher approves and times the

matches. Later children can choose younger wrestling partners.

4. The whistle is a valuable assistant in this activity.

5. Prearrange verbal signals with the children so that a participant can halt the match by using the signal if they need to stop.

*COMMENTS:*

For a variation, place a wide line of tape down the center of the mat. Contestants stand facing each other on the line. When the whistle blows they try to push each other off the line of tape entirely. A foot or hand still on the line counts and the play continues until one of them has no more contact with the tape.

47

## BALL THROW

*MATERIALS:* A box of spongy or foam balls, and a whistle. Use 3 balls for every 2 children. Do this in a large indoor space to allow running.

*GRADES:* K-6

*PROCEDURE:*

1. Seat children in a big circle. Tell them that when the whistle sounds they are going to throw balls at each other (and at you) until the whistle signals "stop".

2. Dump the balls into the middle of the circle, get out of the way and blow the whistle. Grab a couple balls and throw them.

3. Allow 15 minutes or so, then blow the whistle to stop.

4. Every one helps to return the balls to the box.

*COMMENTS:*

There is a good feeling on everyone's part, and a lot of energy expended. For a variation, place a piece of tape down the center of the room dividing it evenly. Form two teams. The team with the fewest number of balls on their side of the tape at the end wins.

## BOPPING

*MATERIALS:* Two socks each with a foam ball in it, or a commercial bopper set, a stop watch, and a whistle.

*GRADES:* K-6

*PROCEDURE:*

1. Sit children in a circle around mat or defined space.

2. Explain that they are going to "bop" each other for 1-2 minutes.

3. No head or face shots are allowed, nor is hitting around genital areas.

4. Select a match and let them go.

5. Blow the whistle to stop.

## PAPER WARS

*MATERIALS:* A large pile of paper that you don't need, (secondhand computer paper is the best), and a large indoor space.

*GRADES:* K-6

*PROCEDURE:*

1. Each child takes a handful of the paper and crumbles it up to make balls. Each child has his or her own pile.

2. While they are doing that, the teacher puts a piece of tape dividing the space in half.

3. Split the children into two groups and sit them in their "base" on either side of the room.

4. The children stand and aim for the other side when the whistle blows. They may not cross the line.

5. If they get hit, they are out and sit on the sidelines.

6. The last two still throwing balls, are "galaxy rulers" (or whatever you choose to call them).

*COMMENTS:*

This will create a big mess and a lot of fun. You can allow the game to be played without children getting "out". Tell them that when the whistle blows twice they are to go steal someone else's supply of balls and the "winner" is the person with the most balls in their corner. Or play it with no winners at all.

## BALLOON STOMP

*MATERIALS:* Two balloons per child, a large indoor space, (or outdoors if enclosed and not windy).

*GRADES:* 2-6

*PROCEDURE:*

1. Blow up balloons before hand, or have older children help.

2. Seat children along the sidelines of the space

3. Turn the balloons loose

4. Turn the children loose

5. The idea is to step on and pop all the balloons. This is a free for all.

6. Make sure you tell them, NO HANDS.

## COMMENTS:

This game provides a very fun and NOISY time for all! Another way to play is to divide children into teams, and have balloons that are two different colors. They try to stomp on the other team's balloons.

A second variation is to tie the balloons onto children's ankles with yarn or other soft string. They are to stomp on other players balloons, while protecting their own.

## PILE ON

*MATERIAL:* Pillows, and cushions (a rug area preferably) and a whistle.

*GRADES:* K-6

*PROCEDURE:*

1. This is an all time favorite of children, between kindergarten and second grade.

2. Seat children around the rug edges.

3. Place the pillows in the middle of the area.

4. Explain the rules: no hitting, pinching, biting, head bumping; only piling on.

5. Select 4-8 children for each round (use your discretion about which children will work, and which ones are better off waiting until the next pile).

6. Blow the whistle. Let them pile onto each other on top of the pillows for 1-2 minutes. How high can it get without the top person sliding off? Keep your eyes on the bottom person(s), they have the right to call "stop" before the timer.

## COMMENTS:

There may be a bumped head or two, but mostly a lot of friendly jostling and laughter. The children may imitate this activity on their own when you do not particularly want them to, so make sure the rule is clear that this activity may only take place with proper supervision and timing. Children who ignore the rule, should be excluded the next time the activity is done. It will usually only take one such exclusion to set the rule firmly.

# PAINT

Painting is a wonderful medium for imaginative exploration and creativity. There are many different types of paints and endless possibilities. Most painting projects are easily set up. Covering the table and floor makes them a breeze to clean up. It is helpful to have an easel set up to supplement art projects. Using primary colors is a wonderful way to teach color mixing.

Finger painting is still fun for school-age children, especially if a variety of paint, paper and surfaces are used. Why not try mixing tempera paint with cold cream to make a fast, different finger paint. Or finger paint with pudding or white corn syrup mixed with food color. Shaving cream is great for finger painting on the table. Add some glitter to make "fancy" finger paint.

## TYPES OF PAINT TO TRY

| | |
|---|---|
| Watercolors | oil paint |
| acrylic paints | water based inks |
| fabric paint | food coloring |
| powdered or | finger paint |
| liquid tempera | poster paint |

### For Texture How About Tempera Mixed With:

| | |
|---|---|
| glitter | salt |
| sand | sawdust |
| crushed egg shells | coffee grounds |

Add condensed milk to make it look shiny.

Try alum to preserve your paint.

### For Scent How About Adding:

| | |
|---|---|
| Oil of peppermint | almond |
| cinnamon | wintergreen |
| vanilla | cloves |

### Extend Tempera With The Following:

| | |
|---|---|
| liquid starch | liquid soap |
| bentonite (see recipe section) | soap flakes |

The soap makes the paint wash out of clothing more easily.

# TRY PAINTING WITH:

| | |
|---|---|
| paint brushes, all types and sizes | Japanese brushes |
| tooth brushes | sponges |
| Q-tips | cotton balls |
| feathers | small tree branches |
| roll-on deodorant containers | popsicle sticks |
| fingers, toes, or elbows | |

## Other Items To Paint With:

| | |
|---|---|
| the grooved wheels of toy cars | string or yarn |
| hands and feet (prints) | kitchen gadgets |
| marbles and golf balls | straws |
| spray and squeeze bottles | eye droppers |
| turkey basters | rollers |
| medical syringes | |

## Why Not Paint On:

| | |
|---|---|
| easels | mirrors |
| walls (murals) | windows |
| large sheets of paper | rocks |
| cardboard boxes | material |
| t-shirts | foil |
| clay | wood |
| sheets | |

# USE A VARIETY OF PAPER:

| | |
|---|---|
| newsprint | newspaper |
| construction paper | watercolor paper |
| grocery bags | rice paper |
| paper plates | tissue paper |
| oaktag | butcher paper |

## Vary The Paper By Changing The:

| | |
|---|---|
| size | color |
| texture | shape |

And by cutting holes or shapes in the center or sides of paper.

52

## MARBLE PAINTING

*MATERIALS NEEDED:* A large box lid or plastic tray, marbles of different sizes or golf balls, primary colors of tempera paint, spoons, scissors and construction paper.

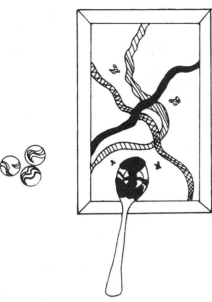

*SET-UP:*

1. Cut the paper to fit inside the box lid.

2. Put the paint into shallow containers.

*PROCEDURE:*

1. Place a piece of paper inside the box lid.

2. Drop a marble into one color of paint and lift it out with a spoon or with fingers.

3. Roll the marble around the box lid by rotating the box.

4. Take out the marble and drop another one into a different colored paint; repeat the process as many times as the child wishes.

*COMMENTS:*

For a distinct pattern use golf balls. Try different sized marbles to compare the effect.

## BUBBLE PAINTING

*MATERIALS NEEDED:* One cup liquid tempera paint, one cup liquid dish soap, water, paper, a large glass jar with a lid, a shallow pan and a straw.

*SET-UP:*

1. Pour the tempera paint and the dish soap into the jar and place the lid on.

2. Mix the two together by shaking.

3. Open the lid and fill with water, close tightly and mix again.

4. Let set overnight if possible.

*PROCEDURE:*

1. Pour mixture into a pan.

2. Each child take turns blowing bubbles.

3. Place paper gently on top of the bubbles, and it will pick up a bubble print!

*COMMENTS:*

This can be done with food color on white paper which makes a lighter design. It is especially attractive on tissue, rice, or other thin paper.

## STRAW PAINTING

*MATERIALS NEEDED:*
Paper, plastic drinking straws, and tempera paint.

*SET-UP:*

1. Put paint in shallow containers.

2. Set out straws and paper for each child.

*PROCEDURE:*

1. Put one end of the straw into the paint and put a finger over the other end. This should draw paint into the straw.

2. Carefully place the straw onto paper still holding the end.

3. Remove finger from the end of the straw and blow the paint onto the paper.

*COMMENTS:*

For an alternative, try using diluted food coloring or water base ink. Cutting the paper long and thin adds an aesthetic dimension to this activity.

## SYRINGE PAINTING

*MATERIALS NEEDED:* Assorted sizes of medical syringes without the needles, tempera paint, newspapers, paint containers and large pieces of construction paper.

*SET-UP:*

1. Dilute the paint with water so that it will run through the syringes. Be careful not to make the paint too watery or it will make a mess.

2. Cover the table with a lot of newspaper.

3. Set out the paper and containers of paint with the syringes.

*PROCEDURE:*

1. Put the narrow top of the syringe (where the needle would go) into the paint.

2. Pull the plunger of the syringe about halfway up. The syringe will fill with paint.

3. Push the plunger and the paint will squeeze onto the paper.

*COMMENTS:*

Food coloring mixed with water and water based inks can also be used. Turkey basters or eye droppers are an alternative. Make sure there is a flat surface to dry these pictures on, because they are very runny.

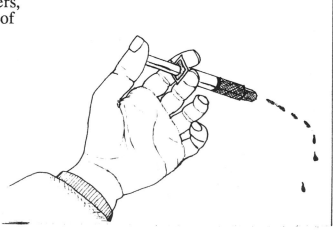

## PAINTING ON THE TABLE

*MATERIALS NEEDED:* Tempera paint, liquid starch, a clean large table, masking tape, paper, and paint brushes.

*SET-UP:*

1. This can be a messy project and should be done outdoors, if possible.

2. Divide the table into painting work areas with masking tape.

*PROCEDURE:*

1. Have children smooth liquid starch on the table top in their work area (or they can just use paint right on the table top).

2. Next put paint on top of the liquid starch.

3. Either use fingers or brushes to paint.

4. Place paper over the picture and rub across the back.

5. Gently lift the paper off the table.

*COMMENTS:*

If words are written, they must be written backwards to print correctly on the paper. Painting directly onto the table top without the liquid starch is not nearly as messy; although it does dry up faster, making the reverse image fainter.

## SHAVING CREAM RESIST PAINTING ON THE TABLE

*MATERIALS NEEDED:* White paper, crayons, shaving cream, blue tempera paint, masking tape.

*SET-UP:*

1. If two tables are available, set one up for the coloring part and set one up outdoors, if possible, for the shaving cream painting.

2. Divide the table up into painting work places with masking tape.

3. On each work place put one table spoon of blue tempera paint and a mound of shaving cream. (Make sure the mixture is light blue, not too dark to cover the crayon drawing).

*PROCEDURE:*

1. Draw a picture with the crayons.

2. When the picture is completed, it is taken over to the shaving cream table.

3. Using hands, mix the shaving cream and paint together and smooth it over the painting space.

4. Carefully, place the picture, crayon side down on top of the shaving cream and press evenly with hands.

5. Make sure that the entire picture has shaving cream/paint over it.

6. Lift the painting off by grasping one corner and hang to dry.

*COMMENTS:*

Other colors of paint can be used for different effects such as white for snow and black for night. Make sure the colors are light enough not to cover up the crayon picture.

**COLOR DRIP PAINTINGS**

*MATERIALS NEEDED:* Spray bottles, food coloring, water, clothespins, construction paper and an outdoor fence.

*SET-UP:*

1. This is a messy project; it is best done outdoors.

2. Fill the spray bottles with food coloring and water. The stronger the color, the better.

3. Hang large sheets of paper on a fence with clothespins spaced far apart, so that paint from one painting does not splash onto another.

*PROCEDURE:*

1. The children spray the colors onto the paper.

2. The colors will blend and run together.

*COMMENTS:*

Large sheets of paper can be used to allow groups of children to create a color drip painting together. For variation, change the intensity, the distance and/or the angle of the spray.

**YARN PAINT FISHING**

*MATERIALS NEEDED:* Primary colors of tempera paint, yarn or string, pie tin or paint dish, straws, paper, hole puncher, newspaper and scissors.

*SET-UP:*

1. Cover the art table with newspaper.

2. Cut pieces of yarn or string about 6 inches long.

3. Punch a hole in the top of each straw and tie on the string or yarn so that it looks like a fishing pole.

4. Put paints in shallow dishes such as pie tins or meat trays.

5. Make sure that there are several straws in each color of paint.

*PROCEDURE:*

1. Children dip the yarn pieces into the paint and drop them onto paper, like drop line fishing. They may use as many colors as desired.

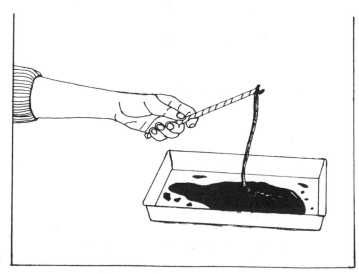

COMMENTS:

The strings may also be put directly onto the paint without the straws.

## YARN PULLING PICTURES

*MATERIALS NEEDED:* Yarn or string, primary colors of tempera paint, construction paper, newspaper and paint dishes.

*SET-UP:*

1. Cover the table with newspaper.

2. Cut yarn or string into different sizes.

3. Put primary colors of paint into shallow dishes.

*PROCEDURE:*

1. Children select the pieces of yarn they wish to use.

2. Dip the first yarn piece into the paint.

3. Place the yarn onto a piece of paper in a design, leaving the end of the string off the paper.

4. Many pieces of yarn can be used on the same picture.

5. Put another piece of paper over the picture.

6. Carefully, place a hand over the paper to keep it in place.

7. Pull the yarn out from the paper, keeping a hand on top.

8. Pick up the top paper and look at both pictures. A colorful design will appear on the top paper.

*COMMENTS:*

A variation is to have the children rub their hands over the top piece of paper; this will squeeze the paint out of the yarn. Then carefully pick the pieces of yarn off the picture.

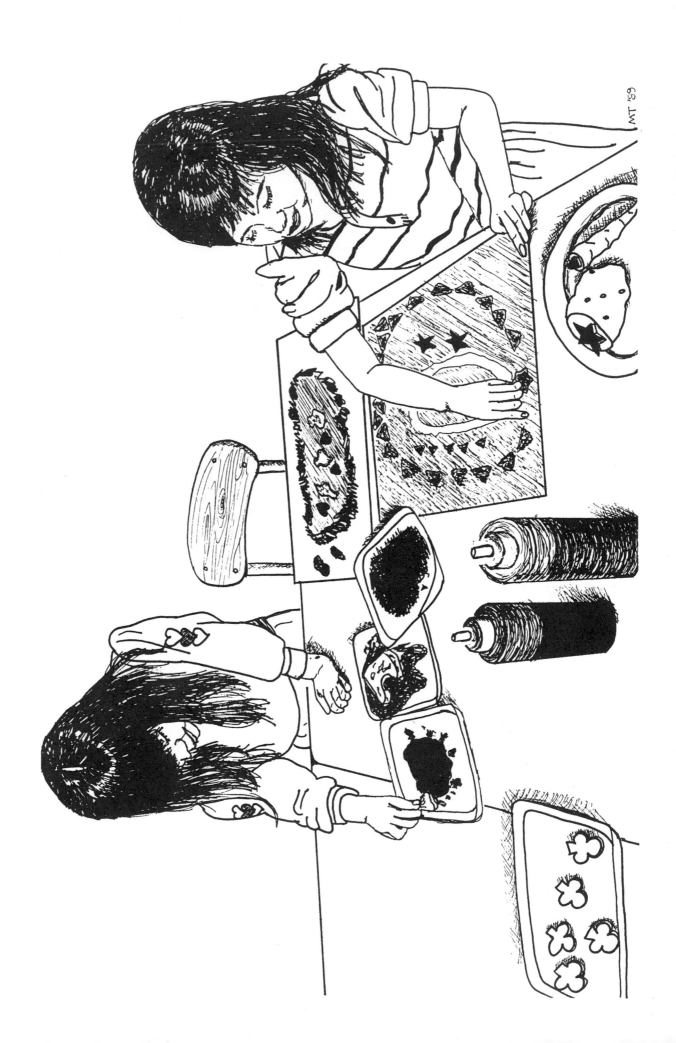

# PRINTING

Printing is an ancient art that began with the Chinese. There are many imaginative ways to print using different methods, textures and designs. Printing can be as simple or as complex as the children desire. Simply dropping paint onto paper and folding it in half is a form of printing. Covering a painting with another piece of paper and lifting it off is another simple print. Complex printing projects include wood block printing and metal etching. In between these is a whole range of printing possibilities.

## TRY PRINTING WITH:

| | |
|---|---|
| tempera paint | water based ink |
| ink | acrylic paint |

## HOW ABOUT PRINTING:

| | |
|---|---|
| cards | stationery |
| pictures | invitations |
| book marks | books |

## TRY PRINTING WITH:

| | |
|---|---|
| sponges | junk objects |
| stencils | styrofoam |
| leaves | yarn |
| fruits and vegetables | wood |
| metal etching | rolling pins |
| rubber bands | rubber pieces |
| stamp pads | Linoleum |

# PRINTING

## TISSUE PAPER PRINTS

*MATERIALS NEEDED:* Multi-colored sheets of tissue paper that bleed, paint brushes, water, scissors, markers, white paper, and newspaper.

*SET-UP:*

1. Put newspaper down to protect the table.

2. Set out pieces of colored tissue paper with scissors, containers of water with clean paint brushes and the white paper.

*PROCEDURE:*

1. Cut shapes or objects out of the tissue paper.

2. Place the tissue paper shapes or objects one by one onto the construction paper and paint over them with water. Be careful not to use too much water because the tissue paper will tear.

3. Peel off the tissue paper and throw it away.

4. The color from the tissue paper will print onto the paper.

5. Children may want to draw on the pictures with markers to complete the project.

*COMMENTS:*

For holiday pictures, have the children cut out pumpkins, eggs, Christmas trees, etc.

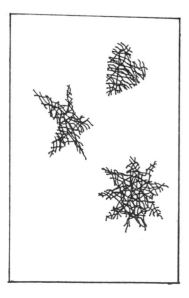

## RUBBER STAMPS

*MATERIALS NEEDED:* Square blocks of wood (approximately 4" x 4"), rubber cement glue, scissors, sheets of rubber material (Doctor Scholls'™ shoe liners, skin diving material or sheets of rubber that have an adhesive back), ink pads, pencils and paper.

*SET UP:*

1. Sand the blocks of wood if necessary.

2. Cut the rubber into squares, a bit smaller than the block size.

3. Put out a piece of rubber, a wooden block, and a pencil for each child.

*PROCEDURE:*

1. Draw a design onto the rubber with a pencil.

2. Cut out the design and either glue or stick it on the block.

3. To print words, make sure to write the letters backwards.

4. For glued rubber, allow at least one hour for drying.

5. Push the stamp onto an ink pad (rainbow pads are fun) and print.

6. Stamping designs onto tissue paper in rows or free-form, makes wrapping paper.

*COMMENTS:*

Children can create very imaginative stamp pads including animals, shapes, and flowers. It is good to make an example of writing words to show them how to write backwards. Sheets of self-adhesive rubber can be ordered from the Ellison Educational catalog, P.O. Box 8209, Newport Beach CA, 92658 (714-646-4498). Cut-up rubber bands can be substituted for the sheet rubber for a different effect.

## LEAF PRINTING

*MATERIALS NEEDED:* Different sized and shaped leaves, tempera paint, shallow paint dishes, paint brushes and construction paper.

*SET UP:*

1. Collect the leaves.

2. Make sure they are not too dry or they will crack.

3. Put paint into shallow dishes.

*PROCEDURE:*

1. Brush paint on the leaves or dip the leaves into the paint. Use many colors on each leaf to make multi-colored prints.

2. Carefully place the leaves, paint side down, onto paper.

3. Rub over the leaf to print.

4. Gently lift off the leaf by the stem.

## FISH PRINTING

*MATERIALS NEEDED:* Several sizes of whole fish, tempera paints or colored ink, paint containers, paint brushes, a bucket of water, washcloth, and light weight paper such as newsprint or imported Japanese paper.

*SET-UP:*

1. Go to your local fish market and purchase several fresh whole fish. It is best to choose a fish with a clear scale pattern.

2. Wipe the fish to remove any moisture or other matter.

3. Ink is easiest but it stains clothing, make sure the children wear smocks.

4. Put tempera paint or ink into containers.

5. Show the children the fish and discuss the ancient Japanese art of fish painting. Examine the fish and explain about its anatomy.

*PROCEDURE:*

1. Brush Paint or ink right on top of the fish with one or more colors.

2. Make sure to cover every part including the fins.

3. Place the paper on top of the fish.

4. Gently but firmly rub hands over the paper touching the entire fish.

5. Carefully lift the paper off the fish.

6. Wash and dry off the fish before printing again.

*COMMENTS:*

This is an old Japanese art. At first the children may think it is offensive to paint on a fish but the results are marvelous! This is great for either a Japanese or sea life theme. The fish skeleton makes an interesting print also. If nontoxic paint or ink is used, the fish can be washed, boned, and then given to a cat to eat.

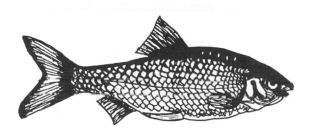

## SPONGE PRINTING OR FRUIT AND VEGETABLE PRINTING

*MATERIALS NEEDED:* Sponges, fruits and vegetables (such as potatoes, apples, avocados, oranges, carrots, and corn on the cob), sharp scissors, sharp knife, paper, tempera paints, liquid starch, and shallow paint dishes.

*SET-UP:*

1. Items to print can be cut in advance by an adult or by the children.

2. Cut shapes out of the sponges or use sponge scraps. For example cut: flowers, sea life, animals, shapes; or hearts for Valentine's day, shamrocks for St. Patrick's Day, and pumpkins for Halloween. For fruit and vegetable painting, cut out similar objects from potatoes or apples, or slice other fruits and vegetables in half leaving in seeds. When carving fruits and vegetables, the object can either pop-out or can be carved inside.

3. Mix liquid starch with paint to make thick paint. Test the print on on newspaper before giving to the children.

4. Put out several colors of paint in shallow dishes.

5. Make sure there are at least two sponges, or fruit or vegetables for every color.

*PROCEDURE:*

1. Dip the sponge or the fruit or vegetables in paint and print on paper.

*COMMENTS:*

This can be done as a year-round project which changes with themes, seasons, or holidays. Also use this process to make wrapping paper.

Pop-up sponges, sheets of thin sponges which pop-up when submerged in water, can be used for a fun alternative. They can be purchased through Ellison Educational catalog, P.O Box 8209 Newport Beach, CA. 92658 (714) 646-4496.

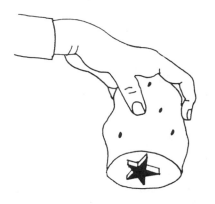

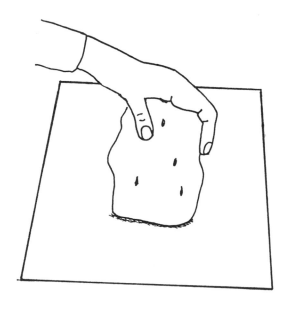
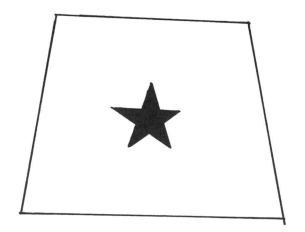

## OBJECT PRINTING

*MATERIALS NEEDED:* All kinds of junk objects such as buttons, bristle blocks, alphabet blocks, sewing machine bobbins, cookie cutters and other kitchen utensils, tempera paint, liquid starch, yarn, masking tape, newspaper and paper.

*SET-UP:*

1. Collect objects from your center and your home.

2. For flat objects, tape a loop of yarn onto the back for a handle.

3. Mix the paint with liquid starch for thickness.

4. Test printing objects on newspaper.

5. Pour paint into shallow paint dishes and put several objects in each color.

*PROCEDURE:*

1. Dip the objects into paint and print them on paper.

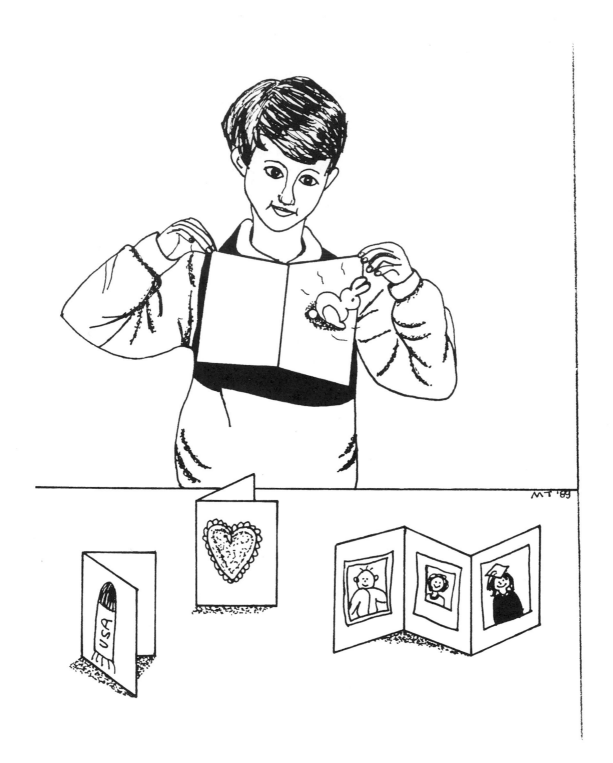

# CARDS

Cards are a creative art project for every season of the year. Children can create many different kinds of cards for family and friends. The children may want to make their own envelopes. This section offers several ideas for cards, but the possibilities are limitless.

Don't limit children to making one card for each holiday or event. Some children like to make many cards and will even develop techniques for mass-production of cards. *The children at our center made a variety of cards and then set-up "The One Stop Card Shop," where they sold cards to parents.*

Creating post cards is also fun. Simply cut out post card sized sheets on heavy paper and draw a place for a stamp and a line down the middle. These can be put out on the art shelf for the children to decorate and write at their leisure.

## CARDS CAN BE MADE FOR ANY OCCASION:

| | |
|---|---|
| holidays | birthdays |
| friendship | special events |
| thank you notes | announcements |
| get well | invitations |

## USE A VARIETY OF PAPER:

| | |
|---|---|
| newsprint | newspaper |
| construction paper | watercolor paper |
| grocery bags | rice paper |
| thin cardboard | tissue paper |

# CARDS

## STENCIL PRINTING CARDS

*MATERIALS NEEDED:* Thin cardboard for a stencil, spray paint or tempera paint with a stencil brush or sponge, construction paper, scissors, newspaper, pens or markers, hole punch.

*SET-UP:*

1. Cover the art table with newspaper, or do the project outdoors.

2. Fold pieces of construction paper into cards.

3. Cut out pieces of cardboard that are the same size as the cards will be.

*PROCEDURE:*

1. Draw an object in the middle of the card board for printing onto the cards. Make sure it is not too large for the cards.

2. Punch a hole in the middle of the picture and insert the scissors; then cut out the object. This makes the stencil.

3. Place the cardboard stencils over the cards and then tape them both to the table.

4. Spray the stencil middle with paint, or dab paint on with a stencil brush or sponge.

5. Carefully remove the tape and lift the stencil off the card.

6. Place the card to dry and continue making cards, as needed.

*COMMENTS:*

For a variation have children use tooth brushes instead of paint brushes. Chalk stencils are also fun to do, but will need to be "fixed" when completed.

## VALENTINE CARDS

*MATERIALS NEEDED:* Red, pink, purple and white construction paper, doilies of many sizes and shapes, pieces of ribbon, yarn and lace, feathers, glitter, sequins, fringe, bangles, stickers, glue, and scissors.

*SET-UP:*

1. Display all of the materials listed above on the art table in an attractive manner.

2. Show some examples of cards children have made in the past. Make sure the correct spelling of Valentine's Day is clearly printed and available for the children to copy.

*PROCEDURE:*

1. Let the children create all kinds of old-fashion Valentine's Day cards.

*COMMENTS:*

This is a great ongoing project. It can be left out for several days in a row, and/or put away and set-up again.

## THREE DECADE CARDS

*MATERIALS NEEDED:* A camera and film, a baby picture of each child, thin cardboard, crayons or markers, rubber cement glue and tape.

*SET-UP:*

1. Send out a notice asking each child to bring an expendable baby picture to school for an art project.

2. Take a picture of each child, (A polaroid camera works well, but the pictures are expensive.)

3. Cut the cardboard into three equal pieces depending on the size you wish for the cards. Older children may cut the cardboard themselves.

*PROCEDURE:*

1. Decorate one side of the first piece of cardboard, for the front cover of the card.

2. On the other side, glue on the baby picture and write pertinent information. For example,"Mary Jones as a baby, born on May 3rd, 1981." Decorate around the picture.

3. On the next piece of cardboard, glue the school picture and write more information. For example, "Mary Jones at after school care, seven years old." Again, decorate around the picture. The back side can also be decorated.

4. On the third piece of cardboard, have the children draw a picture of what they think they will look like when they grow up. Write a sentence to go along with it such as, "This is Mary Jones age 30, she is a famous doctor." Decorate the backside in any manner.

5. Tape the edges of the card to fold like an accordion. First comes the front cover with the card opening into a three fold accordion. Inside the card, the baby picture comes first, followed by the child in the present and ending with the child in the future ( see diagram).

*COMMENTS:*

These cards are delightful to give to parents or other relatives. Children love to see other children's baby pictures; sharing them is a good group time activity. A game can be developed to guess which baby picture belongs to each child.

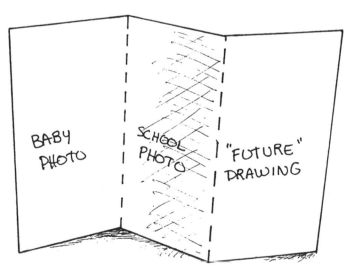

## POP-UP CARDS

*MATERIALS NEEDED:* Construction paper, markers, scissors, tape and other decorations.

*SET-UP:*

1. Put out all material needed for cards on art table.

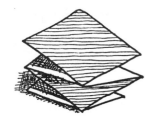

*PROCEDURE:*

1. Have each child select a piece of colored construction paper and fold it over to make a card.

2. Each child must decide what they want to pop-up inside.

3. Draw the pop-up item onto paper, decorate it, and cut it out.

4. Cut out two strips about 1"x4", and fold them together accordion-style.

5. Fasten the middle of the accordion-strip to the back of the pop-up object with tape and fasten the ends to each inside page of the card. The item should lay flat when the card is closed and pop-up when opened.

6. Decorate and write on the rest of the card.

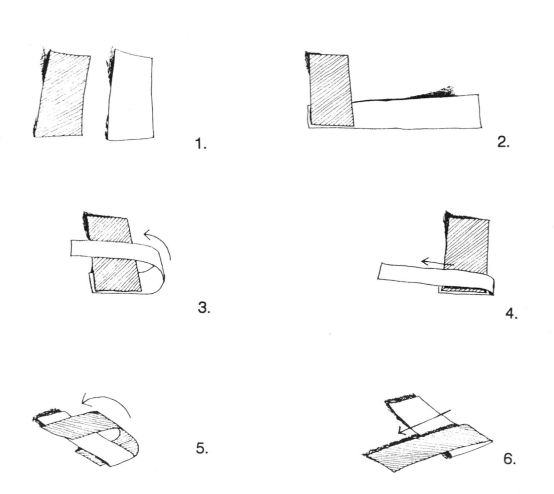

## NATHANIEL'S POP-UP CARDS

*MATERIALS NEEDED:* Construction paper, tape, and markers.

*SET-UP:*

1. Use rectangular paper 8"x2", 3", or 4".

*PROCEDURE:*

1. Fold the paper in half and then in half again.

2. Open second fold and draw on the inside around the crease line (this will be the pop-up object when the card is finished) (see diagram).

3. Open fully and carefully cut out the object around the top and bottom only, leaving sides attached to card.

4. Reverse fold on item (this will make it pop-out).

5. Refold as previously and tape the edge together so that the card cannot open fully again.

*COMMENTS:*

This pop-up card version is best for older children with well developed fine motor skills.

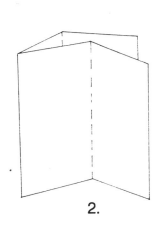

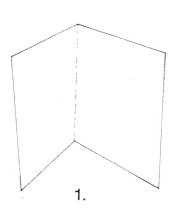

1.

2.

3.

4.

# MASKS

Making masks is a traditional art form. Many ethnic groups use masks for ceremonies and celebrations. Children enjoy pretending to be someone or something else. A good way to achieve this is by wearing masks. There are many ways to create masks, from paper bags and plates to plaster casts of faces. Masks can be worn for dress-up, in plays, in parades, and can be hung up to decorate walls.

# MASKS

# ICE CREAM CARTON MASKS

*MATERIALS NEEDED:* 3-gallon ice cream cartons, masking tape, scissors, cardboard tubes and rolls in a variety of sizes, tempera paint, glue and decorations such as feathers, pipe cleaners, straws, glitter, ribbons, and yarn.

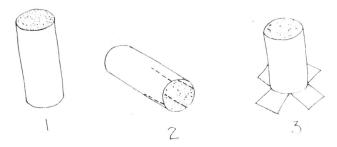

*SET-UP:*

1. Ask your local ice cream store to save containers or ask the children bring them in.

2. If there is a metal rim on the top of the cartons, carefully pry it off. The lid of the carton is not needed but can be cut up for decorations.

3. Set out the materials on the art table.

*PROCEDURE:*

1. Some ideas for masks are a robot, monster, space creature, Hopi Kachina Doll (show pictures as examples), African Masks from different nations (show pictures as examples), ogre and different animals.

2. Using a sharp scissors, cut holes for eyes, nose and mouth. They can be any shape or size depending on what the mask will be.

3. The cardboard tubes can be used for pop-out eyes, nose, ears, or other objects. Cut the tube to the size needed and then cut 4, 1 inch slits, equidistant on the bottom of the tube. Fold them outwards making a platform (see diagram).

4. Tape the tube securely onto the carton so that it is sticking out.

5. Use pipe cleaners, straws, feathers or other objects to make horns, antenna and head dresses.

6. When all the pop-out items are secured, paint the mask using a variety of colors and shapes.

7. Decorate in any fashion.

8. When the mask is finished, have the child try it on. If it is too low, stuff the top with news paper. If it does not rest comfortably on his or her shoulders, cut out sections on either side of the carton for shoulder rests.

72

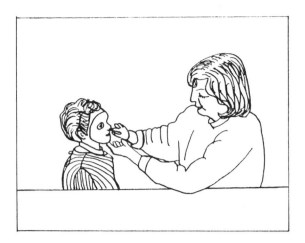

## PLASTER MASKS

*MATERIALS NEEDED:* Plaster of Paris strips, Vaseline, water, a shallow container, paint, head bands or hair fasteners and decorations

*SET-UP:*

1. Cut the plaster strips into 2 to 3 inch long pieces.

2. Purchase or borrow hair fasteners or head bands to keep children's hair away from their faces.

3. It is best to have an adult put the first mask on a child or another adult, to show the children the process. Then the remaining children should choose partners (one creates the mask on the other and then they change places). When children put masks on other children it encourages cooperation and allows for many children to participate at once.

*PROCEDURE.*

1. Fasten hair back, completely away from forehead.

2. Have the child wearing the mask put Vaseline all over his or her face (excluding eyes and lips).

3. Be sure that an adult puts the first mask on a child's face to demonstrate.

4. Place the strips of plaster in the water, and run between two fingers to remove excess water.

5. Gently place the strip on the child's face and smooth down.

6. Leave holes for eyes and mouth.

7. Make sure the strips are placed slightly overlapping and so that no skin shows through.

8. Let the mask dry on the child's face for about 20 minutes. It may itch a bit.

9. Carefully lift the mask off the child's face and let dry overnight.

10. Decorate any way you wish. Paint, feathers and glitter make a wonderful mask!

## PLASTIC BOTTLE MASKS

*MATERIALS NEEDED:* Milk, bleach or other plastic bottles with handles, sharp scissors, glue, decorations such as yarn, foil, glitter, fabric, pipe cleaners, buttons, and marking pens.

*SET-UP:*

1. Cut the back of the container to the handle; do not cut the handle and leave the pour spout intact (see diagram).

2. Set out a wide range of decorations for the children to choose from.

*PROCEDURE:*

1. Have the children draw eyes and mouth on the mask.

2. Puncture a hole in the mask and carefully cut out the eyes and mouth.

3. Decorate, the wilder the better!

*COMMENTS:*

Paint will not stick well on these bottles.

## PAPIER-MÂCHÉ MASKS

*MATERIALS NEEDED:* Newspaper, papier-mâché paste or liquid starch, a round balloon, masking tape, a container to set the balloon in, egg carton, scissors, heavy string or ribbon, and paint.

*SET-UP:*

1. Make sure the balloon is large enough to fit as a mask.

2. Blow up the balloon.

3. Prepare the papier-mâché paste (see recipe section) or use liquid starch.

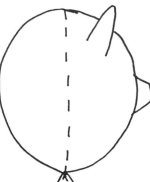

*PROCEDURE:*

1. If the child wants a nose or other parts to stick out, cut up egg cartons and tape them onto the balloon.

2. Follow the directions for Balloon Piñata in the three dimensional art section; making sure to cover the entire

surface.

3. Let dry.

4. Pop the balloon and cut it in half (see diagram).

5. Punch a hole on each side for tying a string to secure the mask on the child's head.

6. Paint and decorate in any manner.

## PAPER BAG MASKS

*MATERIALS NEEDED:* Grocery sized paper bag, scissors, glue, markers, decorations.

*SET-UP:*

1. Set out a paper bag for each child.

2. Put a variety of materials for decorations such as glitter, markers, ribbon, yarn, lace, and pipe cleaners.

*PROCEDURE:*

1. Each child slips the paper bag over his or her head.

2. Have another child mark the places where the child's eyes, nose, and mouth are.

3. Take the bag and draw a face on the mask, using the marks as a guide.

4. Cut out eyes, nose and mouth.

5. Decorate the mask. Fringe can be cut out and glued on.

*COMMENTS:*

Paper bags are also great for fast costumes.

## PAPER PLATE MASKS

*MATERIALS NEEDED:* Paper plates, fabric, sharp scissors, masking tape, glue or a glue gun, a wooden stick or rod, and decorations.

*SET-UP:*

1. If a glue gun is being used, supervise carefully.

2. Place the paper plates, fabric and scissors out on the art table.

*PROCEDURE:*

1. Choose a piece of fabric to cover the paper plate.

2. Trace the plate on the fabric, cut it out and glue the material to the plate (a glue gun works best).

3. Let the glue dry.

4. Cut holes for the eyes, nose, and mouth.

5. Add other details and decorations such as ears, yarn hair, ribbons, material, glitter, or pipe cleaners for antenna.

6. Attach the wooden stick or rod to the back of the plate with masking tape or glue for a handle.

*COMMENTS:*

These make old fashioned masks. They are fun to create and work well for dramatic play, when presenting a favorite story, school plays, special events and shows.

## AFRICAN MASKS

*MATERIALS NEEDED:* Grocery-sized paper bags, crayons, scissors, brushes and thin black paint.

*SET-UP:*

1. Mix the black paint with water to create a wash.

2. Cut an oval the size of a face, out of the front of each paper bag.

3. Show the children pictures of traditional African masks to give them ideas for designs. Show them a variety of masks from the many African nations and let the children decide which style they wish to make.

*PROCEDURE:*

1. Draw shapes for the eyes, nose, and mouth, and cut them out.

2. Color the face of the mask with designs, pressing very hard with the crayons, (geometric lines, wiggles, and shapes work well).

3. Paint the wash of black paint over the mask, making long, even strokes.

4. Let the ovals dry.

5. Cut the four "edges" of the oval. Pull each "edge" back and staple the cut areas (see diagram).

7. The cuts will give the mask a 3 dimensional look.

8. Attach string for wearing as a mask or to hang on the wall.

1. Mask before cutting

2. Making the cuts

3. Stapling cut area

4. Mask after folding and stapling

# PUPPETS

Putting on a puppet show is delightful for children of all ages. There are many ways to create both puppets and a stage, ranging from quite simple to rather complex. Allowing children to make up their own puppets and show is a wonderful learning experience.

Performing a puppet show in front of an audience gives children a chance to develop many kinds of new skills. Some puppet shows take much planning; others can be spur-of-the-moment. For planned puppet shows, there are many roles to fill including: writing or choosing the show, creating the puppets, memorizing the dialogue, planning and making the props and scenery, building the puppet stage and drawing invitations or announcements. Using music in a puppet show is a *wonderful* way to liven it up. *The children in our program performed a puppet show that they chose from a favorite book. They made up an original song to go along with the dialogue.*

Puppet shows provide an excellent opportunity for children to use their imaginations and develop creativity. They are fun projects for interest groups, clubs, or thematic units. Shy children often blossom through the use of a puppet.

## Ideas for making stages

*Large boxes* make impressive puppet stages. Cut a big opening in the front for the stage. Paint and decorate the outside. Suspend the box between two tables; or for marionettes, cut another hole in the top and drop the puppets down. Scenery can be either painted on the back of the box or drawn on rolls of paper. Put one wooden rod on either side of the puppet stage. Attach the scenery paper on both rods so that the different backgrounds can be rolled by. Make curtains out of material over a rope or dowel and tack or tie onto outside or front of the stage. Draping material over a table or a doorway makes an instant puppet stage.

*A shadow puppet show* only takes a few minutes to set up. Tie a sheet across a wall, doorway or from posts. Place a light behind the object to be silhouetted and focus it toward the back of the sheet. Puppets can be cut out of paper shapes or made with hands. For example, sticking up two fingers makes a bunny, or holding out arms and two fingers makes a crocodile with a mouth that opens and closes. Paper shapes should be taped, glued, or stapled to a popsicle stick or tongue depressor.

# PUPPETS

# IDEAS FOR MAKING PUPPETS

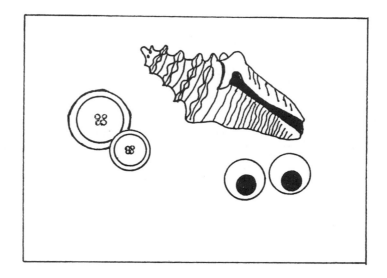

**Decorate puppets with:**
Buttons, acorns, seashells, macaroni, beads, beans, wiggle eyes, yarn, straw, raffia, feathers, felt, material, cotton balls, or sequins.

**Paper cups:** Decorate a paper cup for the body; use either clay or a styrofoam ball attached to a popsicle stick for the head. Make a slit or hole in the bottom of the cup; put the popsicle stick end though it, and you have a *pop-up puppet*.

**Socks, gloves or mittens:** Take old socks, mittens, or gloves and sew, stuff, or cut to create *hand puppets*.

**Cardboard:** Cut out separate body parts such as the head, the trunk, arms, and legs. Paper plates can be used for the body and head. Punch holes in each part and attach with paper fasteners (see diagram). Tie long strings to the top of the head and to both arms and legs. Suspend the strings from a wooden rod or ruler. Decorate by cutting people or animal heads out of magazines or use paint, material or crayons. Wiggle the stick or pull individual strings and you have a *marionette*.

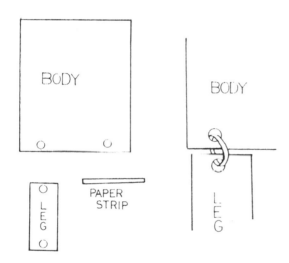

**Finger Puppets:** Make out of soft material or felt. Loosely trace the shape of fingers on material. Draw a border about 1/2 inch from the trace line (see diagram). Cut on the larger border, two of each finger, and sew the two matching shapes together securely. Clip the curves and seam almost to the seam and turn inside out. Decorate with glue and small pieces of material. *Paper finger puppets* can be cut out and fastened around fingers. Create bodies, faces, etc.

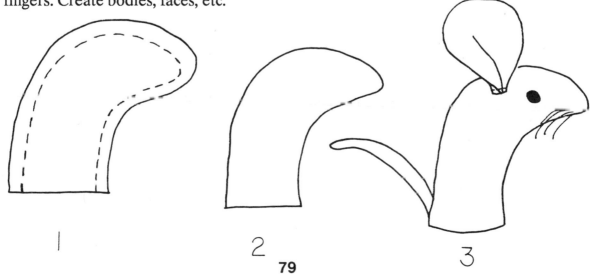

**Paper bags:** Stuff paper bags with newspaper; place a stick or paper-towel roll inside the bag for a handle; and tie the bag at the neck using a string or rubber band. Decorate with markers, yarn, or paint.

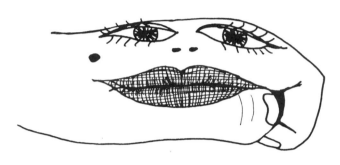

**Hands:** Close fingers tightly into a ball and paint lips onto the thumb and index finger. Use either makeup, face paints or tempera paint mixed with soap. *Hands* can be anything from people faces, animals to scary monsters. Put *acorn* tops or peanut shells on fingertips and draw faces on fingers.

**Wooden rods or sticks:** Attach a styrofoam or clay ball or a paper plate for the head on a wooden rod or stick. Create the face and decorate with hats, hair, ribbons, etc.

**Junk and things:** Puppets can be put together from all kinds of junk items and things around the house or school. Use items such as milk cartons, egg cartons, paint brushes, feather dusters, or plastic bottles. Let the children explore the many different objects they can use to make puppets!

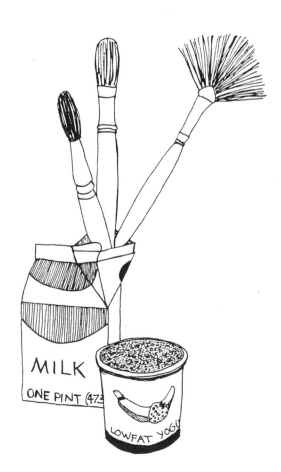

**Papier-mâché:** Glue layers of Paper strips onto wads of newspaper or old light bulbs to make heads for different kinds of puppets. Create arms, hands, fingers, a nose and other body parts, out of papier-mâché or fabric.

**Things found in nature:** Try making a puppet from things collected outdoors such as: sticks, straw, milk weeds, pussy willows, drift wood, shells, and other plants.

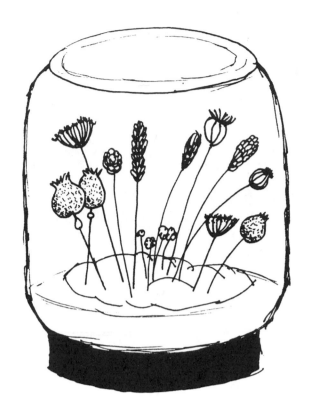

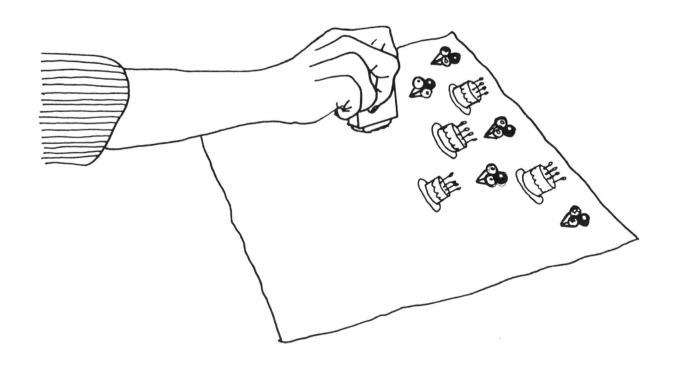

# GIFTS

School-age children enjoy making gifts for family or friends. Parents cherish hand-made presents. There are many gift ideas suitable for school-age children. The following pages are projects that make particularly successful gifts and allow for individual variation.

When children make special art projects to give for presents, hand- made wrapping paper is the perfect finishing touch. There are several easy ways to make wrapping paper. Many forms of printing can be used on tissue paper or light paper to create wrapping paper. See the Printing Section for further information.

# GIFTS

## MOSAICS FLOWER POTS

*MATERIALS NEEDED:* Clay flower pots, ceramic tiles of various colors, tile grout, white glue, white paint, paint brushes, newspaper, a sponge and a cloth.

*SET-UP:*

1. Cover the table with newspaper.

2. Set a flower pot, tiles, and glue with a brush out for each child. Use smaller sized pots for young children.

*PROCEDURE:*

1. Brush a coat of white paint on the rim of the clay pot and let dry completely. (This will make the tiles stick on the pot better).

2. Paint a coat of glue on the back of each tile and place in a row on the rim. Make sure that a small space (1/8-inch) is left between each tile for the grout.

3. Continue until the entire rim is decorated with tiles. Children may want to place tiles on the body of the pot also.

4. Let dry completely.

5. Mix the grout to the consistency of mayonnaise.

6. Using rubber gloves, have the children fill in all the spaces with grout.

7. Sponge off any excess grout on body of the clay pot. Let dry for about 20 minutes and sponge off the excess grout from the tile fronts.

8. Clean the mosaic with a damp cloth after the grout has dried completely.

## EGG SHELL MOSAICS

*MATERIALS NEEDED:* Broken, dyed egg shells, glue, pencils and construction paper.

*SET-UP:*

1. Break up egg shells in medium sized pieces.

2. Place the materials on art table.

3. Children may do paper mosaics first for practice, which is done by drawing a picture and filling it in with small torn pieces of construction paper glued to the paper. This project is an excellent way to illustrate a story.

*PROCEDURE:*

1. Talk to the children about mosaics and show them pictures or examples of tile mosaics.

2. Draw a picture onto the construction paper with a pencil.

3. Fill in with egg shell pieces on top of glue.

## MOSAIC HOT PLATES

*MATERIALS NEEDED:* Ceramic tiles of various colors, tile grout, wood blocks, 1/4 to 3/4-inch pine molding, rubber cement, white glue, a hammer, a pencil, rubber gloves, newspaper, sponge and muffin tin.

1. Break up the tiles by placing them, glaze side down, between several layers of newspaper. Hit them hard with a hammer. Tile clippers can also be used.

2. Have the children sort the tiles by color and put into a muffin tin.

3. Set out a block of wood per child and start with small blocks at first. Frame the wood block with the pine molding, making sure to cut two pieces longer to overlap with the other two strips (see diagram).

4. Show either an example of tile mosaic or pictures from a book.

5. This is an ongoing project, so give at least two weeks to complete.

*PROCEDURE:*

1. Let the children do the egg shell mosaic project or a paper mosaic project first, to get the idea of mosaics.

2. Draw a picture onto the wood, make a very simple design. Fine lines and small details are very difficult to do.

3. Glue the tiles onto the wood with the rubber cement, making sure not to leave large holes. There should be small spaces about 1/8 inch between tiles.

4. Let dry over night.

5. Mix the tile grout to the consistency of mayonnaise.

6. Using rubber gloves, have the children fill in all the spaces with grout.

7. Gently, wipe off all the excess grout from the tiles with a sponge.

8. Let dry completely and clean the surface again with a sponge.

9. If there is grout left on the frame, it can be removed with sandpaper.

*COMMENTS:*

Children can make larger mosaics after they learn the process.

## TISSUE PAPER STAINED GLASS

*MATERIALS NEEDED:* Sheets or scraps of tissue paper, liquid starch, glass containers (jars or bottles), paint brushes, and newspaper.

*SET-UP:*

1. Cover the art table with newspaper.

2. Put out the tissue paper, liquid starch, and glass containers.

*PROCEDURE:*

1. Cut or tear varied colors of tissue paper into small shapes.

2. Brush the tissue paper shapes onto the outside of the glass containers using the liquid starch.

3. Press down loose corners.

4. Cover the glass completely with tissue paper to make a colorful stained glass effect.

*COMMENTS:*

This makes great vases, pencil holders or junk jars. A glue/water mixture can be used in place of the liquid starch. This project can also be done on paper, wood, glass or acrylic sheets, wax paper and even windows.

## LACQUER PICTURES

*MATERIALS NEEDED:* Black paint, tempera paint (bright colors), stiff paper plates, paint brushes, and white glue.

*SET-UP:*

1. Make simple examples to show the children.

2. You may wish to bring in samples of real Chinese or Japanese lacquer objects.

*PROCEDURE:*

1. Paint the paper plate black and let dry, making sure there is no white showing through.

2. Create a brightly colored picture by painting over the dry black paint.

3. Let the picture dry.

4. Paint the surface with a glaze of two parts white glue and 1/2 part water.

5. Let dry and repeat the glazing daily for one week.

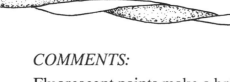

*COMMENTS:*

Fluorescent paints make a bright contrast on black backgrounds. This process can be done on pieces of wood, cardboard and other surfaces.

## CREPE PAPER BOTTLES

*MATERIALS NEEDED:* Sheets of colored crepe paper, scissors, glass bottles, glue, tape and an electric drill.

*SET-UP:*

1. Take the drill bit off; it is not necessary for the project.

2. Place this activity near an electrical outlet.

3. Set-up the art table with glue, crepe paper, and a bottle for each child.

*PROCEDURE:*

1. Cut one-inch-wide long strips of crepe paper.

2. Tape one end of the crepe paper to the head of the drill (an adult should work the drill).

3. Have a child hold the other end of the crepe paper.

4. Turn on the drill and let it twist the paper.

5. The crepe paper will wind tightly to form a colorful rope.

6. Put glue on the bottle and wind the crepe paper rope around the bottle tightly. Start from the bottom and wind up.

*COMMENTS:*

This makes a wonderful vase or pencil holder. Yarn pieces can also be wound around bottles for a similar effect.

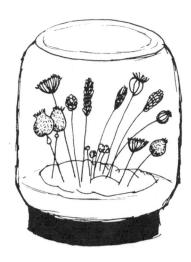

## FLOWERS IN A JAR

*MATERIALS NEEDED:* Baby food jars and lids, modeling clay, small dried flowers, scissors, glue and felt.

*SET-UP:*

1. Set-up the art table with a jar, flowers, balls of clay and felt.

*PROCEDURE:*

1. Trace the jar lid on felt and cut out.

2. Cover the outside of the jar lid with the round piece of felt (also the inside of the lid if desired).

3. Stick a ball of clay onto the inside of the lid.

4. Cut the flowers to fit inside of the jar; then press the stems into the ball of clay making a flower arrangement.

5. Put the lid onto the jar and carefully tape around the outside edge to secure the lid.

6. Set the jar upside-down so that the flowers stand up.

*COMMENTS:*
These are quick, easy projects and are enjoyed by all age groups. They can also be created in larger bottles or jars.

## CLAY EGG HOLDERS

*MATERIALS NEEDED:* Clay, large and medium hard-boiled or blown eggs, acrylic paints and brushes.

*SET-UP:*

1. Purchase clay that can either be air-dried or oven baked, or make your own clay (see Recipes Section).

2. Hard boil the eggs.

3. For blown eggs, prick a hole in the top and bottom of the eggs and blow out the insides. Set aside for use when holder is finished.

4. Prepare art table for clay work.

*PROCEDURE:*

1. Make a lump of clay the size of a large egg.

2. Flatten the clay into a 3/8 inch thick oval.

3. Place a large egg in the middle of the clay.

4. Form different types of animals, objects, or people around the egg.

5. Some ideas are: a bear, a frog, a bunny, a snail, a swan, a nest, and a person. Push clay through a garlic press to make hair, a nest or other details.

6. Remove the egg often, to make sure it does not stick to the clay, or lightly oil the egg.

87

7. Make sure the clay has a flat bottom and holds the egg firmly.

8. Let the clay dry without the egg, or oven bake. Most clay will shrink when dried.

9. Paint the egg holder when completely dry.

10. Dye or paint the medium sized blown egg or hard-boiled egg, and place in the holder.

## COMMENTS:

The only use for the large egg is during the making of the holder. The reason for this is because the clay shrinks when drying and will not hold a large egg. The smaller egg will actually be placed into the holder when it it dry.

## APPLESAUCE/CINNAMON ORNAMENTS

*MATERIALS NEEDED:* 4 ounces ground cinnamon, 10 tablespoons applesauce, mixing bowl, wax paper, rolling pins, a spoon, acrylic paints, small paint brushes, ribbon or string, a variety of cookie cutters, rolling pins, a cookie sheet and an oven.

## SET-UP:

1. Set-up places to roll out dough onto wax paper.

## PROCEDURE:

1. For Applesauce/cinnamon dough do the following: Measure out about 10 tablespoons of applesauce and put in a mixing bowl; then add about 4 ounces of ground cinnamon. Mix it together with a spoon and knead into a ball. The dough should be moist, so add more applesauce, if needed. The cinnamon works like flour. Sprinkle it on the dough and rolling pin if they get sticky.

2. Roll out the dough onto the wax paper.

3. Press the cookie cutters into the dough or cut with a knife.

4. To avoid breakage keep the ornaments smaller than 4 inches.

5. Punch a hole towards the top of the ornaments, place them on the cookie sheets, and bake at 200° for 20 to 30 minutes.

7. Let cool on a wire rack.

8. Paint with acrylic paints.

9. Put string or ribbon through the hole for hanging.

## COMMENTS:

These ornaments smell wonderful and should last for a few years. It also makes the school smell great! Store them in a box lined with tissue paper and keep in a cool, dry place. Tempera paint works also, but acrylic paint has more luster.

## BAKER'S DOUGH MAGNETS

*MATERIALS NEEDED:* Baker's dough (see Recipes Section), acrylic paint, roll of stick-on magnets (purchase at a crafts store), cookie cutter, cookie sheets, and wax paper.

## SET UP:

1. Make the Baker's dough with the children, according to recipe.

2. Put out balls of dough on wax paper.

3. Have cookie cutters or clay tools ready.

## PROCEDURE:

1. Make things out of the dough either by hand or with cookie cutters.

2. When finished, place the objects carefully onto the cookie sheet.

88

3. Gently push a small strip of magnet into the back of the object, making it as even as possible with the edge of the dough. Be sure to put a big strip of magnet on large objects, or the magnet will not hold the dough.

4. Bake according to directions.

5. When cooled, paint the front side.

## WOODEN MAGNETS

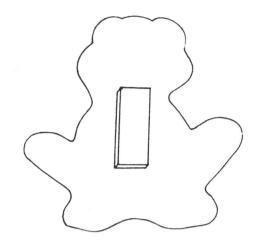

*MATERIALS NEEDED:* Very small light pieces of wood (shapes work well) that are sanded (order from a crafts catalog or get from the lumber yard), a roll of stick-on magnet strips, a metal mirror or another metal surface, glue, glitter, paint, sequins or other decorations.

*SET-UP:*

1 Put out the pieces of wood, the glue and the decorations.

2. Keep the magnet strips away from the table until the project is finished.

*PROCEDURE:*

1. Pick out wooden pieces or shapes and glue them together.

2. Then decorate the wood shapes from a wide variety of materials.

3. Let them dry.

4. Cut out a piece of magnet from the roll, making sure it is large enough to hold the wooden pieces on metal.

6. Secure magnet strip to the back of the wood. Display the finished products on the mirror.

*COMMENTS:*

The magnets can be displayed on refrigerators at home or used to hold up art work. They sell well at crafts fairs or fundraisers.

## MAGNET CREATURES

*MATERIALS:* Empty walnut shells, magnetic strips, paint, felt, plastic eyes, glue,paper, scissors, and a hole puncher.

*SET-UP:*

1. Crack the walnuts in halves and take out the fruit inside, it can be saved for snack time or baking projects.

2. Put out the materials and allow for free choice.

3. Cut the felt into small squares, a bit larger than the nuts.

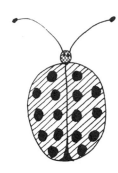

*PROCEDURE:*

1. Talk to the children about different ideas for creatures.

2. Cover the open side of the walnut with felt.

3. Glue the felt and trim the edges.

4. Decorate the top of the walnut shell to create animals, monsters, and people. Some examples are:

> a. Paint red and let dry; use black hole-punching for spots; draw or make wings and use wire for antennas; and you have a lady bug.

> b. Paint walnut and let dry; attach eyes; draw face; use wire for whiskers; make ears from felt; and you have a cat.

> c. Glue on many eyes; furry fabric; and paint for a monster.

5. After the creature has dried, attach a magnetic strip to the back.

# CANDLE MAKING, WAX AND CRAYONS

Candle making is very enjoyable for children. Paraffin wax can be purchased in large slabs from catalogs or hobby stores. Metal and rubber molds can also be purchased, but milk cartons and other inexpensive materials work just as well. Wicks can be bought from a hobby store or from art catalogs. The best wicks have wire inside. Be sure you use real wicks, or test your string, because some string does not burn. If you do use string, dip the pieces in wax and let dry before putting them in the candles. Below is basic information for easy candle and wax preparation; please refer to it when doing a project.

## BASIC STEPS FOR CANDLE MAKING PREPARATION

**1.** Wax should be chopped-up into small pieces using a hammer and chisel. Children enjoy helping with the wax chopping. It is best to chop the wax in advance, because it does take time.

**2.** **Make sure the melting of the wax is well supervised.** An adult should do the pouring. Talk to the children about fire safety and explain why they must have an adult supervise them when they burn their candles at home.

**3.** When melting wax, it is safest to use a double boiler. Use an old pan that is large enough to fit a coffee can inside. Put about two to three inches of water inside the pan and place it on top of the burner. When the water starts to boil, place the can of wax inside. Make sure the water does not evaporate while the wax is melting.

**4.** Stir the wax as it melts, and do not let it get too hot. Take the wax off the boiler as soon as all the pieces are melted.

**5.** Crayons can be used to color the wax. Peel crayon stubs and carefully drop them into the wax while it is melting, making sure not to splash the wax. Stir the crayon stubs until the color has mixed evenly.

**6.** Measure the wick to about six inches longer than the mold. Wind it around a pencil or stick; place it in the center of the mold; and lay the pencil across the mold (see diagram on page 95).

**7.** The top layer of wax often gets an air pocket that looks like an indentation. This can be filled using warm wax.

# CANDLE MAKING, WAX AND CRAYONS

## SAND CANDLES

*MATERIALS NEEDED:* Wax, crayon stubs, a double boiler, sand, a sand table or box, foil and wicks.

*SET-UP:*

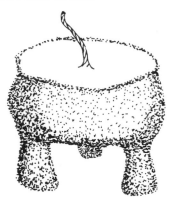

1. Set up a double boiler and follow the directions for candle making preparation.

2. If you do not have a sand box or a sand table, line a large box with foil and fill it with sand.

3. Wet down the sand.

*PROCEDURE:*

1. Have children use their hands to make a hole in the sand for the candle. Flatten the sand on the bottom or the candle will not sit up to burn; or press fingers into the sand, to make legs. Round shapes such as circles, ovals and hearts work well.

2. Melt the wax and stir in a crayon stub for color.

3. Carefully pour the wax into the sand hole.

4. Put the wick into the middle of the candle and hold up until the candle starts to harden.

5. When completely hardened, pull the candle by the wick, out of the sand.

6. Brush off the excess sand, leaving a sandy coat.

*COMMENTS:*

This is a fast easy candle to make. Children can experiment with different shapes and sizes. It is a good first candle making project for younger children.

## COLORFUL SAND CANDLES

*MATERIALS NEEDED:* Wax, crayon stubs, a double boiler, wicks, colored sand (or mix powered tempera with sand or salt), baby food jars, clear plastic glasses, or cups, and pointed sticks.

*SET-UP:*

1. Set up a double boiler and follow the directions for candle making preparation.

2. Prepare the colored sand by either purchasing colored sand at a craft supply store or making your own. Use either white sand or salt, mixed with 1/2 teaspoon of dry powered tempera paint.

3. Set out the containers.

*PROCEDURE:*

1. Pour a layer of colored sand or salt into a container.

2. Tilt the container to create wavy layers of sand.

3. Continue pouring layers of colored sand or salt.

4. A pointed stick can be used to swirl the colors and mix the layers.

5. Fill the container 3/4 full.

6. Melt the wax with a crayon.

7. Push a wick into the middle of the sand and tie the end onto a pencil; rest it across the container.

8. Pour melted wax on top to seal the sand and let it harden.

*COMMENTS:*

To make a paperweight, use a baby food jar with a lid and follow steps 1-6 and 8. Cover the top of the lid with felt and place it on the jar. Carefully turn the jar upside down onto the lid.

## PAPER CUP OR MILK CARTON CANDLES

*MATERIALS NEEDED:* Wax, crayon stubs, waxed containers for molds, wicks, double boiler, and pencils.

*SET-UP:*

1. Set up the double boiler and follow the directions for candle making preparation.

2. Choose a mold for the candles.

*PROCEDURE:*

2. Melt the wax and add crayons for coloring.

3. Carefully pour the wax into the mold.

4. Place the wick in the center of the candle, with one end tied around the pencil and rest it on the mold.

5. After the candle has hardened, peel off the mold.

*COMMENTS:*

Dixie cups, paper cups, and milk cartons make good molds and the different sizes help adjust the project to the amount of wax on hand. If you use metal molds, grease them first or spray with silicon mold release. For multicolors and layers, pour one layer and let dry, then pour the next layer until the candle is at the desired height. To make a candle with holes, pour wax over crushed ice cubes. Another variation is to make chunks of colored wax in an ice cube tray. After they harden, place them in the mold and pour slightly cooled clear wax over them.

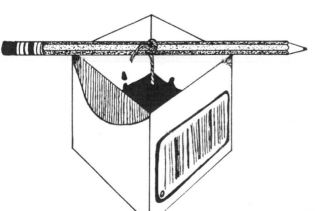

## FRIED EGG CANDLE

*MATERIALS NEEDED:* Wax, wicks with wire inside, a yellow crayon, a double boiler, mixing cups, stirring sticks, and aluminum foil.

*SET-UP:*

1. Set up a double boiler and follow the directions for candle making preparation.

2. Set out a mixing cup and a stirring stick for each child.

3. Cut a piece of foil for each child.

*PROCEDURE:*

1. Melt the wax (about 2 ounces per child).

2. Color the wax yellow with the crayon.

3. Pour 2 ounces of the yellow wax into each cup.

4. Let the children stir the wax constantly until it becomes the consistency of clay. Remind them that the wax is still hot.

5. Have the children carefully take the wax out of the cups and form balls around a piece of wick. The ball should be about 2 inches across.

6. Flatten one side of the ball so that it will sit up. It will resemble an egg yoke.

7. Place the "yoke" on the piece of foil, making sure the wick is sticking straight out of the center of the yoke.

8. Fold up the edges of the foil, forming a circle around the "yoke." Leave about 1 1/2 to 2 inches from the yoke to the edge of the foil.

9. Next melt some clear wax in a clean pot or can.

10. Let the clear wax cool for a few minutes and test it by pouring a small amount on the "yoke," making sure it does not start to melt.

11. Then carefully pour the clear wax around the yoke and let it harden.

12. When the wax has hardened, peel off the foil.

## ROOT BEER FLOAT CANDLES

*MATERIALS NEEDED:* Wax, a glass mug or soda fountain glass, a brown crayon, an old hand mixer, a double boiler, wicks, root beer scent (if you can find it at a candle or hobby store), pencils, and straws.

*SET-UP:*

1. Set up a double boiler and follow the directions for candle making preparation.

2. Experiment with the wax to find out how much is needed to fill a mug or glass approximately 3/4 full, and then prepare enough wax to fill all the children's mugs or glasses.

*PROCEDURE:*

1. Melt enough wax to fill each mug 3/4 full.

2. Color the wax with a brown crayon.

3. Drop in scent (optional).

4. Carefully pour the wax into the mug.

5. Tie the wick to the center of a pencil. Set the pencil horizontally across the mouth of the mug, so that the wick hangs down the center of the mug.

6. Insert the straw, when the wax has started to form a film on top.

7. Let harden.

8. Next, melt the clear wax and let it cool for a few minutes.

9. Put the hand mixer into the melted wax and whip until the wax thickens, becomes white and looks like foam.

10. Remove the pencil, leaving the wick sticking straight up.

11. Top the root beer candle with the whipped wax. It will look like foam.

Make sure the wick is sticking through the foam.

12. A cherry for the top can be made by molding warm red wax into a ball.

*COMMENTS:*

This project may be too expensive if you buy mugs or glasses for all the children. Check with local bars or restaurants for old mugs, or look for bargains at garage sales and variety stores. These make great presents and fundraisers!

## WAXED HANDS

*MATERIALS NEEDED:* Paraffin wax, a bag of ice, a bucket, crayon stubs, large coffee can, hot plate, a pan, an old large spoon, and a hot pad.

*SET-UP:*

1. Set up a double boiler and follow the directions for candle making preparation.

2. Prepare a bucket of ice water about 2/3 full.

*PROCEDURE:*

1. Fill the coffee can with wax chunks about 3/4 full.

2. Drop in several crayons to color the wax.

3. Put the can inside the double boiler pan and melt the wax, stirring occasionally.

4. When the wax has melted, carefully set the coffee can on the hot pad and let it cool somewhat.

5. Children's fingers must be slightly bent but no fists.

6. Two children at a time can make wax hands by dipping their hands first into the ice water for a count of three and then dipping it into the melted wax for a count of three.

7. Continue until there is a wax buildup of 1/8" to 1/4".

8. Let the wax on their hands cool for 20 minutes. As the wax cools, it will expand.

9. Slowly pull the wax off the hand.

*COMMENTS:*

This project needs lots of supervision. Do not over cook the wax. Younger children can do a wax finger instead of a hand.

**CRAYON PRESSINGS**

*MATERIALS NEEDED:* Old crayons, wax paper, an iron, cheese grater, or knife, scissors, hole punch and yarn.

*SET-UP:*

1. Put pieces of wax paper down on the table.

2. Give each child a cheese grater or a knife for shaving. Give children instruc-

tions on how to use the grater or knives safely.

3. Peel the paper from the crayons.

4. Put the iron on a medium setting and assure proper supervision.

*PROCEDURE:*

1. Let the children choose many crayons to shave.

2. Grate or shave the crayons onto the wax paper, leaving about 1" border around the sides.

3. Cover the crayon shavings with another piece of wax paper.

4. Have an adult or an older child, iron over the wax paper until the crayons melt.

5. When the pictures have cooled off, let the children cut the edges for decoration.

6. Punch a hole; string with yarn to hang in the window.

*COMMENTS:*

During autumn, add colorful leaves to the crayon shavings. Also pieces of construction paper, feathers and other decorations can be pressed in between the wax paper.

## SANDPAPER CRAYON TRANSFER PICTURES

*MATERIALS NEEDED:* Small pieces of coarse sandpaper, crayons, light-colored paper or cloth, and an iron.

*SET-UP:*

1. Put the iron on a medium setting and assure proper supervision.

2. Put newspapers down on the surface of the ironing board or table.

3. Do a simple example with the children watching.

*PROCEDURE:*

1. Draw a picture onto the sandpaper by making heavy marks with the crayons. Writing must be backwards to transfer correctly.

2. Put the sand paper, picture-side down onto a piece of paper or cloth. The cloth must be about the size of the sand paper or bigger.

3. Cover with newspaper and iron evenly over the sand paper. The iron must be hot enough to melt the crayons.

4. After ironing, peel up a corner of the sandpaper to see if the picture is transferring, if not keep going.

5. The picture will transfer from the sand paper onto the paper or cloth and take on the texture of the sand paper. The picture will still be left on the sand paper, so the children will have two copies to keep.

*COMMENTS:*

Make sure you use an old iron, because if wax gets on the iron it can be considered "dead" for ironing clothing.

## MELTED CRAYONS DESIGNS

*MATERIALS NEEDED:* Candles in holders, long crayons, newspapers, rubber bands, and construction paper.

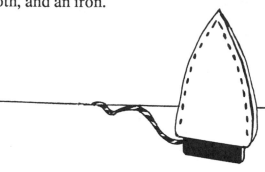

*SET-UP:*

1. This project needs very close adult supervision and is best done with older children.

2. Cover the table with newspaper, wax is difficult to remove.

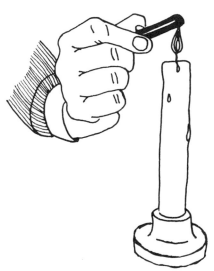

3. Place one candle for every two children in the center of the table.

4. Peel off the paper from the crayons.

5. Put out construction paper and the peeled crayons.

*PROCEDURE:*

1. Children simply hold the tip of the crayon in the flame of the candle for a few seconds until the crayon begins to drip.

2. Bring the crayon back over the paper and let the melted wax drip onto the paper, creating a design.

3. Change colors often.

## COMMENTS:

Remember to put long hair into rubber bands and tie it back. Be sure there is plenty of adult supervision. Make sure the crayons are long enough not to burn any fingers.

## MORE CRAYON MELTING

*MATERIALS NEEDED:* A warming tray or waffle iron, crayons, foil, and paper.

*SET-UP:*

1. Plug in the warming tray or waffle iron.

2. Peel the paper off the top half of the crayons.

*PROCEDURE:*

1. Put children's name on a waiting list.

2. Have children come up one at a time to the warming tray or waffle iron.

3. Draw a picture right onto the tray with the crayons, *or* place a piece of foil on the tray first and draw a picture on top of the foil.

4. Put a piece of paper over the tray (or foil) and press gently for a lift off.

*COMMENTS:*

Use an old warming tray as it will get very messy. The wax will wash off easily with hot water and cloth. For a similar effect, use the griddle side of a waffle iron. The waffle side can be used to make a rubbing-type melting project.

## RECYCLING CRAYONS

*MATERIALS NEEDED:* Old crayon stubs, a muffin tin or other containers, and an oven.

*SET-UP:*

1. Peel the paper off the crayon stubs.

2. Put out the muffin tin.

3. Pre-heat the oven at 400° for ten minutes.

*PROCEDURE:*

1. Sort out the crayons into the muffin tins.

2. Mixing colors will create a rainbow crayon.

3. **TURN OFF THE OVEN.**

4. Put the muffin tin into the oven and let the crayons melt.

5. Let cool and the crayons will pop out. To speed up the cooling process, put the muffin tin in the freezer.

6. Children can draw pictures with the fat crayons.

*COMMENTS:*

The tins can be cleaned easily with hot water and soap. Try using metal chocolate molds as a variation.

## MELTED CRAYON SWIRL PICTURES

*MATERIALS NEEDED:* A hot plate, crayon stubs, thin cardboard, a stick, metal spoon or nail, a shallow baking pan or cookie sheet, and a pair of pliers.

*SET-UP:*

1. Heat water in the pan until hot (not boiling).

2. Peel off the paper from the crayon stubs.

3. Cut cardboard pieces or heavy paper that fit inside the pan.

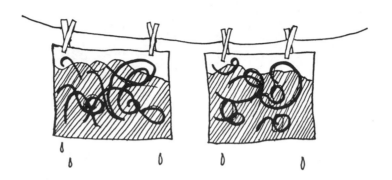

*PROCEDURE:*

1. Drop the crayon stubs into the water.

2. Let the colors melt.

3. Swirl the melted wax with a stick, spoon, or nail.

4. Next, take each piece of cardboard and fold back one corner.

5. Grasp the fold with the pliers and carefully dip the cardboard into the water. The crayon swirls will lift off the top of the water and onto the cardboard.

6. Let the cardboard dry on a clothes line.

# THREE-DIMENSIONAL ART

There is a distinct developmental progression in children's work with materials that can be used three-dimensionally. The stages follow the same development as those in block building, from flat laid-out designs, to hesitant second story building, into full-fledged three-dimensionability. Presenting materials and watching children create will tell a teacher a lot about each child's stage of growth. Allow room for differences.

## SOME COMBINATIONS OF MATERIALS

**1.** Soaked peas, or marshmallows, and toothpicks on a cardboard base.

**2.** Raisins and colored toothpicks on a foil-covered cardboard base.

**3.** Carrot slices and any of the above combinations. These can be done at snack time and then eaten.

**4.** Styrofoam packing materials or dough can be substituted for the food items.

**5.** Straws and paper clips. Bend the clips to form straight, corner, or angled joints. Pull the ends of the clips out to tighten the connections.

**6.** Paper cups and paper clips. Glue can be used to hold the mouth of the cups together; clips can be used for edges.

**7.** Small pieces of wood and glue.

**8.** Recycled aluminum cans, thin wire, and model cement.

**9.** Toothpicks and glue. Since building upward requires good small muscle coordination, this is recommended for older children. Fifth and sixth graders are capable of some very elaborate creations. The strongest building shape is the triangle; lots and lots of triangles are very sturdy when connected. For best results, the children should start with a flat base and build upward from it.

**10.** Tongue depressors and glue make great houses, bird feeders, boxes with lids, frames, and a variety of sculptures.

# THREE-DIMENSIONAL ART

## ALUMINUM FOIL FIGURES

*MATERIALS:*
Aluminum foil
and scissors.

*SET-UP:*

1. Cut varied
sized rec-
tangles from
the foil.

*PROCEDURE:*

1. Warn the children that the sharp
edges of the foil can cause cuts.

2. Give children a rectangular-shaped
piece of foil.

3. Have the children watch as the
teacher does a step-by-step demonstra-
tion.

4. Cut the foil as shown (see diagram).

5. Crumble sections 2 and 3 first to
form the arms. They should be
crunched long and skinny (see
diagram).

6. Crumble section 1 for the head. It
should be pushed together into a ball.
Do this carefully so the connection between head and arms does not rip.
(This caution is the same for all remaining sections.)

7. Crumble section 4 and then 5 for the
legs. Turn them up at the bottom for
feet.

8. The last section to
crumble is the body (it is
the center part left over).
Be extra gentle with this
part.

9. Once all sections are
crumbled and formed, the
figure can be shaped into
postures and motions.
These can be anything ap-
propriate that the children
want to make; running, sitting, climbing, playing, etc. Animals
can also be made out of these basic
cuts; just turn them onto their feet.

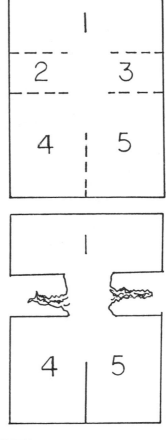

*COMMENTS:*

This project produces a collection of
strange and exotic creatures to line a shelf
or display area. As a variation, have the
children work together to create a farm or
football team. It can also be used for
storytelling and used with a moonscape or
space theme. Finished products can also
be painted.

## PAPER ROLL PICTURES

*MATERIALS:* Thin strips of colored
paper, scissors, paper glue, pencil,
newspaper and regular construction paper
(8 1/2" x 11".)

1. Cover the table with newspaper.

2. Place strips in long thin containers within reach of children.

3. Give each child a piece of construction paper for the base of the design.

*PROCEDURE:*

1. Cut a strip to any desired length. Roll it over the pencil tightly.

2. Let it stay there for a minute, then slide the pencil out.

3. Glue the roll of paper onto the construction paper anywhere.

4. Do another strip the same way, varying the length and color.

5. In this way, cover the paper completely, in patterns, stacked up, etc. This project produces light, airy, colorful and interesting designs that look very modernistic.

## NEWSPAPER ROLL GEOMETRIC STRUCTURES

*MATERIALS:* a large stack of newspapers, and rolls of masking tape.

*SET UP:*

1. This project should be done with grades 3-6, and can take several days to complete.

2. Explain to the children about polyhedrons before starting this project, especially hexahedrons (six faces) and octahedrons (eight faces), three and four sided pyramids (tetrahedron and pentahedrons) and cubes. This does not have to be a very involved talk, just enough to familiarize them with the terms.

3. Showing a few examples is helpful. However, do not tell them this is a geometry project until after they have completed their structures.

4. Put the children into pairs or groups of four. Each group will make its own structure.

*PROCEDURE:*

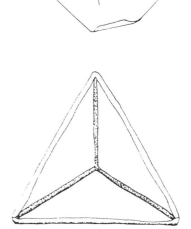

1. Put two sheets of newspaper together, flat on the table.

2. Roll them as tightly as possible, starting with one corner and rolling toward the diagonally opposite corner. This takes practice and patience, because the tighter the roll, the stronger the structure will be. There should be a corner edge in the center of the long roll for the roll to be best. Tape to hold.

3. Make a large pile of these rolls.

4. Begin to tape the ends of the rolls together in angles and shapes, starting with a basic flat shape. These can be triangles, squares, or any other shape the children decide to use. There should be a flap on each end of the rolls that is perfect for taping to another roll.

5. Add to the flat shape by building upward, or out.

6. Allow the children to create any type of shape they want.

7. When the group is finished, ask them to count the number of faces (open areas) and sides (newspaper rolls). The number of faces tells them the name of their shape.

8. The completed structures can be painted, or the faces covered with tissue paper and starch.

*COMMENTS:*

Hang the geometric structures from the ceiling around the school. They will make a delightful addition, and a real hands-on math experience.

Tetrahedron    4 △ faces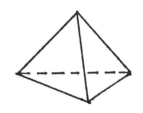

Hexahedron    6 □ faces

Octahedron    8 △ faces

Dodecahedron    12 ⬡ faces

Icosahedron    20 △ faces

## Regular polygons
(all sides and angles equal)

mCogley
89

# Polyhedrons
## (many faces)

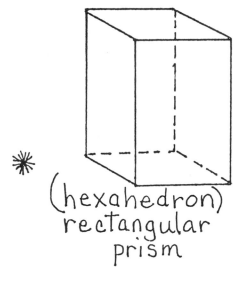

(hexahedron)
rectangular
prism

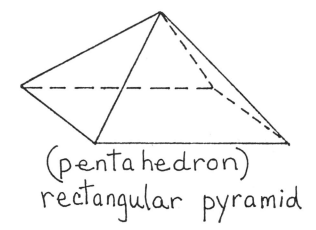

(pentahedron)
rectangular pyramid

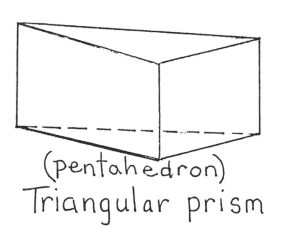

(pentahedron)
Triangular prism

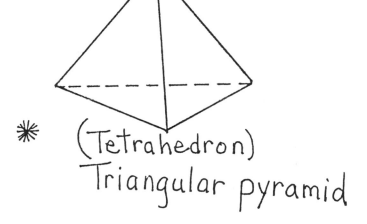

(Tetrahedron)
Triangular pyramid

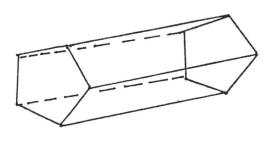

pentagonal prism

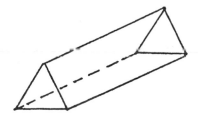

Equilateral triangular
prism

* regular polyhedron

mCogley
89
**107**

## HANGING ANIMALS OR OBJECTS

*MATERIALS:* Very large paper or material (2 ft x 4 or 5 ft is good), staples, cotton or newspaper stuffing, marking pens, crayons, or fabric paint, and scissors.

*SET-UP:*

1. Decide on a theme for the animals or objects such as cactus plants, whales, dinosaurs, pumpkins, etc..

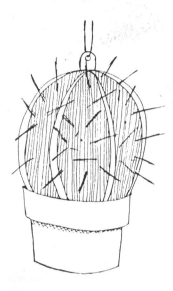

*PROCEDURE:*

1. Draw large animals or shapes on the paper or fabric. For paper, cut out two of the pattern. For fabric, place the pattern on FOLDED material and cut it out.

2. Make certain that the sides fit together correctly.

3. Decorate one side of both pieces of the animal or object. (Let dry if fabric paints are used.)

4. Put the two sides together, and staple most of the way around the shape, leaving a section undone. (Sew, if using cloth.)

5. Stuff the shape with newspaper wads, cotton, shredded paper, or packing materials.

6. Finish stapling or sewing the sides together.

7. Use tape to reinforce the top in one or two sections. Punch a hole through the tape, and run a string or yarn through. Hang from the rafters or ceiling. If the shapes or animals are too big to hang, prop them up in corners or on chairs.

*COMMENTS:*

Fabric shapes can also be made smaller and used as pillows. Fabric glue is available in crafts shops.

## YARN MOSAIC DESIGN PICTURES

*MATERIALS NEEDED:* Colored balls of yarn, scissors, paper, newspapers, glue, and pencils.

*SET-UP:*

1. Cover the table with newspaper.

2. Put out balls of yarn, scissors, pencils and paper for each child.

*PROCEDURE:*

1. Have children draw a picture on the paper with a pencil. Remind them to make the picture simple with large spaces and little detail.

2. Using pieces of cut yarn, fill in the design or picture.

3. For older children, glue each piece of yarn down separately. For younger children, glue a small section of the picture and then press down pieces of yarn.

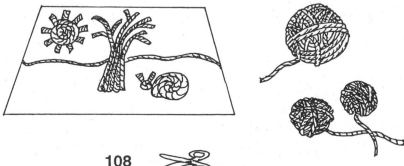

## COMMENTS:

This is a time-consuming project. It can be worked on and put away for another time. The more complex the design, the longer it will take to finish.

## STRING BALLOON BALLS

MATERIALS NEEDED: Small balloons, string, liquid starch, white glue, containers to hold the balloons (baby food jar, yogurt container, margarine cup), and newspapers.

### SET-UP:

1. Cover the table with newspapers.

2. Mix liquid starch with glue (about four parts starch to one part glue) and put in a shallow dish.

3. Blow up the balloons and prop them on or slightly inside of containers.

4. Cut strings to workable lengths for children.

### PROCEDURE:

1. Soak the string in the starch/glue combination.

2. The children wind each string tightly around the balloon, leaving spaces in between. The smaller the spaces, the more sturdy the finished ball will be.

3. After the entire balloon is wrapped with string, let the ball dry over night.

4. Pop the balloon and pull it through an opening.

### COMMENTS:

The string ball is fun for games of indoor catch. However, it is fragile. Yarn can also be used, but the starch/glue should be applied both by dipping and by using a paint brush. Yarn can be glued and coiled around the balloon without leaving a spaces. In this case the balloon will shrink inside after of few days of sitting.

## OJO DE DIOS — GOD'S EYES

MATERIALS NEEDED: Two ice cream sticks or tongue blades, sticks, twigs or pencils; and colored yarn or string.

### SET-UP:

1. Have the children roll the yarn into balls. This is easier to work with than skeins of yarn which tangle easily.

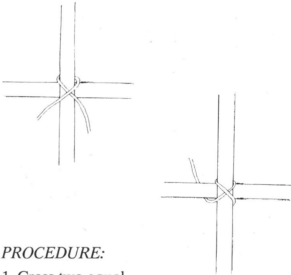

### PROCEDURE:

1. Cross two equal-sized sticks in the middle.

2. Tie a knot with the yarn around the center of the sticks where they cross (see diagram).

3. Weave the yarn over the top stick, around the underside, then over the stick again. Pull the yarn toward the next stick and repeat (see diagram).

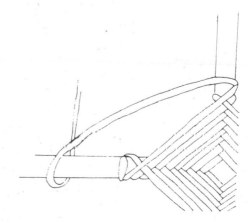

4. Continue weaving around the crossed sticks, clockwise.

5. Change colors by tying the new color onto the old one.

6. The ends can be decorated by hanging yarn pieces, tassels, feathers or beads.

## COMMENTS:

Ojo de Dios means "eye of God" in Spanish. God's Eyes were often made as good luck pieces. Even the kindergarteners can do this project successfully. Try using other types of materials such as fibers, ropes, and rug yarn.

## BALLOON PIÑATA

*MATERIALS NEEDED:* A balloon, papier-mâché or liquid starch, toilet paper roll, newspapers, tissue paper, masking tape, paint, pencils, glue, candy or small toys to fill the piñata.

## SET-UP:

1. Mix the papier-mâché paste (see recipes section) or use liquid starch.

2. Put newspapers down on the table.

3. Find a container to rest the balloon on while applying the papier-mâché.

## PROCEDURE:

1. Blow up the balloon and tie.

2. Tear the newspaper into small strips approximately 1" wide.

3. Moisten the newspaper strips with papier-mâché paste or starch, and wrap them smoothly around the balloon.

4. Cover the balloon so that no spaces are left, except for the tied end.

5. Let the balloon dry overnight; then put on one more coat of papier-mâché.

6. Twist a piece of newspaper into a rope to make a handle. Dunk the ends in papier-mâché paste or starch and lay each end on the top of the paint and secure it with masking tape. Or reinforce the tie end of the balloon and when dry punch a hole in the reinforced area on each side. Run a sturdy string through to support piñata.

7. After it has dried completely, decorate the piñata with small squares of tissue paper; wrap squares around the eraser end of a pencil and stick with glue onto the piñata. Or cut tissue paper into strips that are about 4" wide; fold and cut to make frills or fringe. Paint may also be used.

8. When dry, pop the balloon; fill the piñata with candy/and or prizes, and close with tape.

9. Hang the handle from a rope and use as you would a regular piñata.

## COMMENTS:

Newspapers dipped in liquid starch can be substituted for the papier-mâché paste for a quicker process. Make sure you start this project at least one week before your party day (unless you are in a very dry climate), because it does take several days to dry. Also make sure the handle is sturdy and firmly attached. Hang the piñata from a pole with a long string. Blindfold the children and let them swing at the piñata with a bat or stick. Move the piñata up and down with the string, to make it more challenging for the older children. It is important to make a rule that no one is may jump and grab the treasure when it finally spills because this can cause injury. *In our program we have the children retrieve the treasure in small groups, each taking an equal amount of prizes.*

Piñatas can be used for many holiday celebrations and also for themes such as dinosaurs and space. Large and small balloons and other items such as toilet paper and paper towel rolls and cardboard tubes can be put together to make animal shapes. For a really quick piñata, a cardboard box can be substituted for the balloon.

110

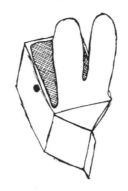
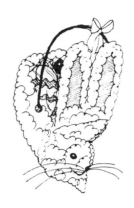

## BUNNY BASKETS

*MATERIALS NEEDED:* 1/2 pint milk or orange juice cartons, construction paper, a marking pen, a hole punch, long pipe cleaners, sharp scissors, glue, and cotton balls.

*SET-UP:*

1. Place the milk carton on its side and trace the ears (see diagram).

2. Cut out the ears. Teachers and older children should cut out ears of each carton in advance.

3. Punch out two holes on either side of the head for the handle.

4. Make an example to show the children.

*PROCEDURE:*

1. Glue the cotton balls onto the milk carton until it is covered completely (except the bottom).

2. Make eyes, whiskers, and inside of ears with construction paper and glue onto bunny basket.

3. Attach the pipe cleaners into the holes for the handle.

## PAPER PLATE RABBIT

*MATERIALS NEEDED:* Two paper plates per child, scissors, stapler, pink, blue, and black construction paper, pipe cleaners, markers, cotton balls and glue.

*SET-UP:*

1. Trace the ears and bow-tie on paper plates (see diagram).

2. Set out the materials on the art table.

3. Make a simple example.

*PROCEDURE:*

1. Cut out the ears and bow tie from the paper plate and staple them to the other paper plate (rabbit head).

2. Cut out insides of the ears from pink construction paper.

3. Glue the insides of the ears in place.

4. Glue down cotton balls, covering the ears (except where pink is), and the head.

6. Cut eyes and whiskers from construction paper or use pipe cleaners for whiskers.

7. Decorate the bow tie.

8. Encourage the children to make the rabbits as individual as possible.

111

## NATIVE AMERICAN SAND/MUD PAINTING

*MATERIALS NEEDED:* Sand, powered tempera paint, mud, cardboard, pencils, scissors, glue and paint brushes.

*SET-UP:*

1. Mix about 2 cups of sand (white sand works best), cornmeal, or salt with 1/2 teaspoon of dry powered tempera paint to color.

2. Take the children on a nature walk to collect different types of soil. Let the mud dry out.

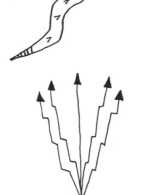

3. Cut out cardboard pieces.

*PROCEDURE:*

1. Draw a simple design on the cardboard with a pencil. Native American symbols make interesting designs. Fill in the design with glue.

2. Sprinkle colored sand or dried mud over glue.

3. Let dry.

*COMMENTS:*

There are several symbols that Native American use for religious purposes. It is not respectful to use these symbols in art projects. However, there are many symbols that are not religious (see diagram). Children may want to make use these symbols, or design their own.

## MORE SAND PAINTING

*MATERIALS NEEDED:* 25 lb. white sand, food coloring, rubbing alcohol, and large boxes.

*SET-UP:*

1. Divide the sand into 5-6 equal parts, depending on how many colors you wish to use. Place each part into a separate box.

2. Mix 1/2 cup alcohol with about a tsp. of food coloring.

3. Add this mixture to a box of sand and stir thoroughly. This works best if it is done by hand, but the food coloring will stain hands.

4. Color each box of sand a different shade.

5. Allow them to dry completely. The alcohol will dry very quickly, especially if the sand is stirred occasionally.

6. The more food coloring used, the brighter the sand will become. Do NOT use water, it takes too long to dry.

*PROCEDURE:*

1. Same as preceding project.

*COMMENTS:*

This method using food coloring and alcohol instead of powered paint is preferred by some teachers because the dried sand is not as messy and is more permanent. However, the sand must dry completely first. The colors are more natural than using powdered paint.

# EXAMPLES OF USEABLE SYMBOLS

Mountains

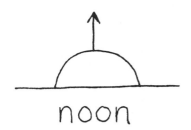

noon

Bear Alive

water

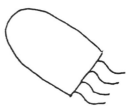

Bear dead

buffalo country

deer

rain

Among

mCogley
89

# GRAHAM CRACKER HOUSES

*MATERIALS NEEDED:* At least 6 Graham crackers per child, eggs, powdered sugar, cardboard squares, foil, masking tape, and lots of types of candy and other sweets such as: red hearts, wafer cookies (doors), spice or gum drops, life savers, gummy bears and worms, mints, hard candies, pretzels (windows), M & M's, kisses, candy canes and peppermint sticks, marshmallows, chocolate chips, sprinkles, candied fruit slices, and small cookies.

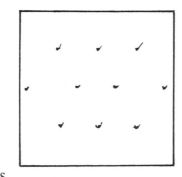

*SET-UP:*

1. Cut squares of cardboard and cover them with foil for bases. Put a piece of tape on one corner for names. Small houses should have at least 6 X 6 inch bases.

2. Younger children will need at least four whole crackers for a small house. Older children will want to make bigger houses and will need more crackers. Allow at least eight crackers each, but they may need more. Some houses can go into second and third stories!

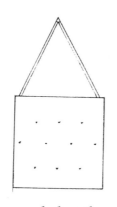

3. Separate the egg whites from yolks. Mix 4 egg whites with a pound of powdered sugar, until creamy. This amount will serve as the "glue" for approximately four houses, depending on their sizes.

4. Divide available candies into equal amounts per child and put aside until frame is dry.

*PROCEDURE:*

1. For a small house, break all crackers in half.

2. Put a small amount of "glue" in the center of the foil base. Place one half of a cracker flat on the glue. This is the floor.

3. Dip all four sides of each cracker part into the "glue", and wipe off the excess. These are the walls and they are stood up along the side of the floor of the house. Balance them on each other for support and let them sit a while.

4. Dip another cracker piece in "glue" and place it flat on top of the sides to make the ceiling. Let this sit a while also.

5. Now the roof. Dip opposite sides of two cracker halves into the glue and carefully place them on the ceiling to form the roof (see diagram). Let the whole house dry overnight.

6. The next day, have the children decorate the houses by dipping the candy pieces into the glue and placing them around the house and yard in interesting designs.

*COMMENTS:*

These houses are edible, and delightful to look at. Grown-ups love them! However, they are susceptible to ants, hungry siblings, pets, and sometimes parents. Don't wait too long to eat them.

Larger houses take more planning and teach a lot of architectural techniques. Children can create anything from California flat-roof houses with patios, to four story apartment buildings. When possible, let the parents help with the cost of making these.

# RECIPES

This section includes a variety of simple art recipes to make at school. It is a great way for children to learn about measurement, mixing ingredients, the cooking process, and how different art materials are made.

There are several home made clay and dough recipes. To color or decorate, food coloring can be added to water when mixing the ingredients. This will make the whole batch of dough one color. Food coloring can also be added after the ingredients have been mixed but before they are kneaded. Take the amount of dough or clay desired, add a few drops of food coloring, and knead. This allows for multi-colored clay.

After the clay or dough has either been dried or baked, paint can be used to decorate the objects. Acrylic paint works best. A clear gloss finish can be applied over the dried paint to add shine. Tempera paint can also be used. White glue mixed in with tempera makes the paint more glossy.

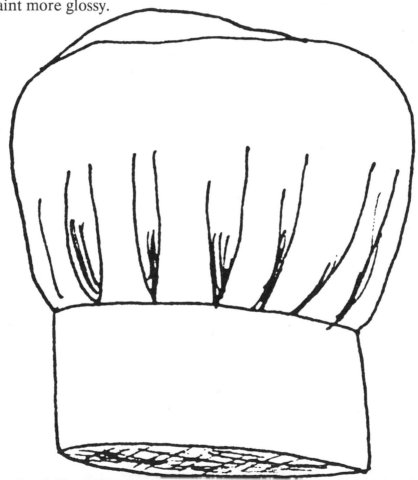

## RECIPES

## WHITE BREAD CLAY

*INGREDIENTS:*

- 8 slices of day old white bread
- 1/2 cup of white glue
- 1 tablespoon glycerin

*HOW TO MAKE IT:*

**1.** Cut the crusts off the slices of white bread.

**2.** Crumble the bread into little pieces.

**3.** Place them in a bowl and mix them with the glue and glycerin.

**4.** Using your hands, mix the bread and glue together until they form a sticky clay-like blob.

**5.** Form a large ball of clay and take it out of the bowl.

**6.** Dust a clay board with flour before gently kneading the dough.

**7.** When it begins to get smoother, knead harder.

**8.** Continue kneading for about 5 minutes, until the clay is smooth and not very sticky.

**9.** Keep the dough wrapped tightly in plastic, when not in use, and store in the refrigerator.

**10.** The dough begins to harden very quickly when exposed to air. If this happens, add small drops of water to the dry dough.

**11.** Air dry the dough on wax paper for several days. Turn the objects over from time to time to prevent sticking and to let them dry evenly.

**12.** The clay can be baked in an oven at 300° for 15 to 20 minutes. This will make the clay a brownish color.

**13.** When the clay is dry, it can be decorated.

## HOMEMADE CLAY

*INGREDIENTS:*

- 6 cups baking soda
- 3 cups cornstarch
- 3 and 1/2 cups water
- 1/2 cup salt

*HOW TO MAKE IT:*

**1.** Stir all the ingredients together in a saucepan.

**2.** If desired, add food coloring to the water.

**3.** Cook on medium heat, stirring occasionally, until the mixture bubbles and thickens.

**4.** Spoon out the clay onto a board and cover with a damp cloth.

**5.** After the clay has cooled, knead it until smooth.

**6.** To store the clay, roll it into small balls, and poke a hole in the top of one. Fill the holes with water and place the clay in a plastic container with a lid, or in a tightly sealed plastic bag. Keep the clay in the refrigerator.

**7.** The clay will slowly air dry.

## MODELING CLAY

*INGREDIENTS:*

- 1 cup corn starch
- 3 cups white flour
- 2/3 cup water
- 1/2 cup cold water

*HOW TO MAKE IT:*

**1.** Pour salt and the water in a sauce pan.

**2.** Stir over medium heat for 4-5 minutes; then remove from the heat.

**3.** Combine the corn starch and the cold water together and pour into the sauce pan.

**4.** Stir the mixture together until it is smooth.

**5.** Return the sauce pan to the burner and cook until thickened.

**6.** Air dry the completed objects.

## BAKERS DOUGH

*INGREDIENTS:*

- 4 Cups white flour
- 1 cup salt
- 1 1/2 cups water

*HOW TO MAKE IT:*

**1.** In a large bowl, combine flour and salt until well mixed.

**2.** Stir in 1 cup of water and continue to mix.

**3.** Slowly add the remaining water to the mixture and turn the dough in the bowl.

**4.** Flour a working surface and knead the dough for ten minutes or more.

**5.** If the dough is too dry, wet your hand and continue kneading and if the dough is too wet, mix 1/4 cups of both salt and flour and sprinkle on the working surface. Continue to knead allowing the salt and flour to mix into the dough.

**6.** Wrap the dough in plastic, when you are not using it.

*BAKING INSTRUCTIONS:*

**1.** Bake the clay projects on a cookie sheet in a regular oven.

**2.** To prevent sticking, dust the cookie sheet with flour.

**3.** Bake at low heat 250 to 300°.

**4.** To check if the items are baked enough, let them cool slightly and press down gently. If they are pliable, they must be cooked longer. If they do not move when pressure is applied, they are done. The time will vary with the size and thickness of the do ugh. Begin by baking the items for 20 minutes and checking them. Check the larger items every 30 minutes.

**5.** Let the dough objects cool before decorating.

## GLUE-DOUGH

*INGREDIENTS:*

- 1/2 cup flour
- 1/2 cup white glue
- 1/2 cup cornstarch

*HOW TO MAKE IT:*

**1.** Mix all the ingredients together in a bowl.

**2.** If the mixture is too dry, add glue; if it is too sticky, add flour.

**3.** Store the dough in a margarine tub while working with the dough.

**4.** The dough is air dried overnight.

## DOUGH

*INGREDIENTS:*

- 1 cup flour
- 1/3 cup salt
- 1/2 cup water
- a few drops of liquid detergent or vegetable oil

*HOW TO MAKE IT:*

1. Combine flour and salt together in a large bowl.

2. Slowly add the water into the flour/salt mixture by stirring with a spoon.

3. If too dry, add a bit of water, and if too wet, sprinkle with flour; then knead.

4. When all ingredients have been mixed together, put down wax paper sprinkled with flour for the dough kneading.

5. The dough will harden in the air. When not in use, store in tightly-closed plastic containers or bags. To keep for a week, store in refrigerator.

## COOKED DOUGH

*INGREDIENTS:*

- 2 cups baking soda
- 1 1/2 cups water
- 1 cup cornstarch

*HOW TO MAKE IT:*

1. Combine ingredients in a large bowl.

2. Add food coloring to the water for color.

3. Mix with a fork until the mixture is smooth.

4. Place in a pot and boil over moderate heat until it thickens.

5. Let cool and spoon onto wax paper.

## SOAP DOUGH

*INGREDIENTS:*

- 1/2 cup liquid starch
- 4 tablespoons salt
- 1 cup liquid soap
- 1/8 cup water
- 2 cups cornmeal

*HOW TO MAKE IT:*

1. Mix the food coloring with the liquid starch for color.

2. Combine all the materials in a large bowl.

3. Put out pieces of wax paper.

4. Give each child a ball of soap dough.

5. Let the dough creations air dry.

## NATURAL DOUGH

*INGREDIENTS:*

- 1 cup flour
- 1/2 cup salt
- 1 cup water
- 2 tablespoons vegetable oil
- 2 tablespoons cream of tartar (optional)
- beet, spinach, or carrot juice for coloring

*HOW TO MAKE IT:*

1. Combine the salt flour and oil together in a large mixing bowl.

2. Slowly add the water.

3. Cook over medium heat.

4. Stir the mixture until the dough becomes stiff.

5. When cooled, knead the dough until it feels smooth.

6. Add a few drops of the vegetable juices for coloring. The beet juice will make pink dough, the spinach juice,

green dough, and the carrot juice, orangish yellow dough.

**7.** Store the dough in tightly closed plastic containers or bags in the refrigerator.

## CHINESE STYLE DOUGH

*INGREDIENTS:*

- 3 1/2 cups white flour
- 1 1/2 cups sweet rice flour (also known as glutinous rice flour; purchase at Asian food stores)
- 7 teaspoons salt
- 4 teaspoons honey
- 1 3/4 cup water

*HOW TO MAKE IT:*

**1.** Combine both types of flour and salt in a large mixing bowl.

**2.** Boil the water and mix in 1 1/2 cups.

**3.** Slowly add 1/4 to 1/2 cups more boiling water. The mixture should be fairly dry; it should bind together but not be sticky.

**4.** Form the dough into a flat lump and steam for 30 minutes.

**5.** When steamed, break into small lumps and cool on a rack or on a towel.

**6.** When cooled, knead in 4 teaspoons of honey, a bit at a time.

**7.** Color by adding a few drops of food coloring or powered tempera paint when kneading.

**8.** Knead into dough. Keep wrapped tightly in a plastic bag or covered with a damp towel.

**9.** This clay retains it shape without shrinking, and air dries into a strong, hard clay. It can be used to make delicate projects. Artists in China use this dough to make colorful clay figures.

## PAINT EXTENDER

*INGREDIENTS:*

- 1 cup bentonite (bentonite powder can be purchased at art supply stores),
- 1/2 cup powdered soap,
- 2 quarts water

*HOW TO MAKE IT:*

**1.** Mix the ingredients together with an egg beater or in a blender.

**2.** Place in a plastic or ceramic container for about 2-3 days.

**3.** Stir the mixture once each day.

**4.** Mix a few tablespoons of the extender with one part powdered tempera paint, 2 parts soap and 2 parts liquid starch. If it is too thin, add more liquid starch and if it is too thick, add water.

## OIL-LIKE PAINT

*INGREDIENTS:*

- Powdered tempera paint (one part)
- liquid dishwashing detergent (two parts).

*HOW TO MAKE IT:*

**1.** Mix the paint and detergent together until it makes a very thick and creamy paint.

**2.** Use a popsicle stick to spread the paint onto paper.

**3.** Paint in layers to look like real oil paint.

## QUICK FINGERPAINT RECIPE

*INGREDIENTS:*

- 1 cup liquid starch
- 1 cup liquid tempera paint
- 1 or 2 spoonfuls of powdered soap

*HOW TO MAKE IT:*

**1.** In a shallow paint container mix the above ingredients until smooth.

**2.** Spoon onto finger paint paper, shelf paper, or directly onto the table.

## ANOTHER QUICK FINGERPAINT RECIPE

*INGREDIENTS:*

- Wallpaper paste (wheat paste)
- tempera paint
- lukewarm water

*HOW TO MAKE IT:*

**1.** Mix the wallpaper paste with lukewarm water until smooth.

**2.** Keep mixing and adding the paste until you have the desired thickness.

**3.** Add the tempera paint and mix together.

## COOKED FINGERPAINT

*INGREDIENTS:*

- 1 cup cornstarch
- 2 cups of cold water
- 2 envelopes unflavored gelatin
- one cup powdered soap

*HOW TO MAKE IT:*

**1.** Dissolve the cornstarch in 1 1/2 cups of cold water.

**2.** Soak the gelatin in the remaining 1/2 cup of cold water.

**3.** Combine the two.

**4.** Cook over medium heat, stirring from time to time. The paint should become thick and glossy.

**5.** Mix in the soap and stir well.

**6.** Add powdered paint, or a few drops of food coloring, and store in jars with lids.

## MORE COOKED FINGERPAINT

*INGREDIENTS:*

- 1 1/2 cups laundry starch
- 4 cups boiling water
- 1/2 cup talcum powder
- 1/2 cup powdered soap
- food coloring or tempera paint

*HOW TO MAKE IT:*

**1.** Mix the starch with cold water until it is thick and creamy.

**2.** Add the boiling water to the mixture, stirring constantly until it becomes transparent.

**3.** Cook the mixture and add 1/2 cup soap flakes and 1/2 cup talcum powder. Stir until they are well mixed.

**4.** Add tempera paint or food coloring.

**5.** Beat with an eggbeater until the paint is smooth and thick.

**6.** Store in the refrigerator in plastic containers.

## SOAPY PAINT

*INGREDIENTS:*

- 2/3 cup powdered soap
- 1/3 cup of water
- food coloring

*HOW TO MAKE IT:*

**1.** Combine the soap and water in a large mixing bowl.

**2.** Add a few drops of food coloring if a color is desired, or leave white for snow or cloud pictures.

**3.** Whip with a hand eggbeater or an electric mixer.

**4.** Paint onto paper with a sponge or use a popsicle stick.

## CHALK

*INGREDIENTS:*

- 2 tablespoons of powdered tempera paint
- 1/2 cup water
- 3 tablespoons of plaster of Paris
- small paper cups

*HOW TO MAKE IT:*

**1.** Mix together all the ingredients.

**2.** Pour into a paper cup.

**3.** Let harden for an hour or so.

**4.** Peel away the cup.

## PASTE

*INGREDIENTS:*

- 1/2 cup water
- one cup flour

*HOW TO MAKE IT:*

**1.** Simply mix the two together in a bowl.

## WHEAT PASTE

*INGREDIENTS:*

- 1 1/2 cups boiling water
- 2 teaspoons wheat flour
- 1/2 teaspoon salt

*HOW TO MAKE IT:*

**1.** Simply mix the ingredients together and store in a plastic or glass jar with a lid.

## PAPIER-MÂCHÉ PASTE

*INGREDIENTS:*

- 1 cup non-rising wheat flour,
- 1/4 cup sugar,
- 1 quart warm water

*HOW TO MAKE IT:*

**1.** Mix together flour and sugar in a saucepan.

**2.** Stir in a small amount of warm water.

**3.** Stir constantly and bring to a boil.

**4.** Cook until it is thick and clear.

**5.** Use when warm for best results. Tear small strips of newspaper and dip into paste mixture for papier mâché projects.

**6.** Wallpaper paste (follow the directions on the box) or liquid starch one part starch mixed with 1/2 parts glue, both make good papier-mâché mixtures.

## OOBLECK OR GOOP

*INGREDIENTS:*

- Cornstarch
- powdered tempera paint (optional) or food coloring
- water

*HOW TO MAKE IT:*

**1.** Pour the cornstarch into a large plastic tub.

**2.** Slowly add water that has been mixed with food coloring or a few tablespoons of powdered paint.

**3.** Mix together while adding the water until it is wet but not runny.

**4.** The mixture is ready when it feels dry to the touch but will become wet and runny when squeezed in a child's hand.

**5.** This mixture will dry overnight. Simply add water to resuscitate until it is too dirty to use.

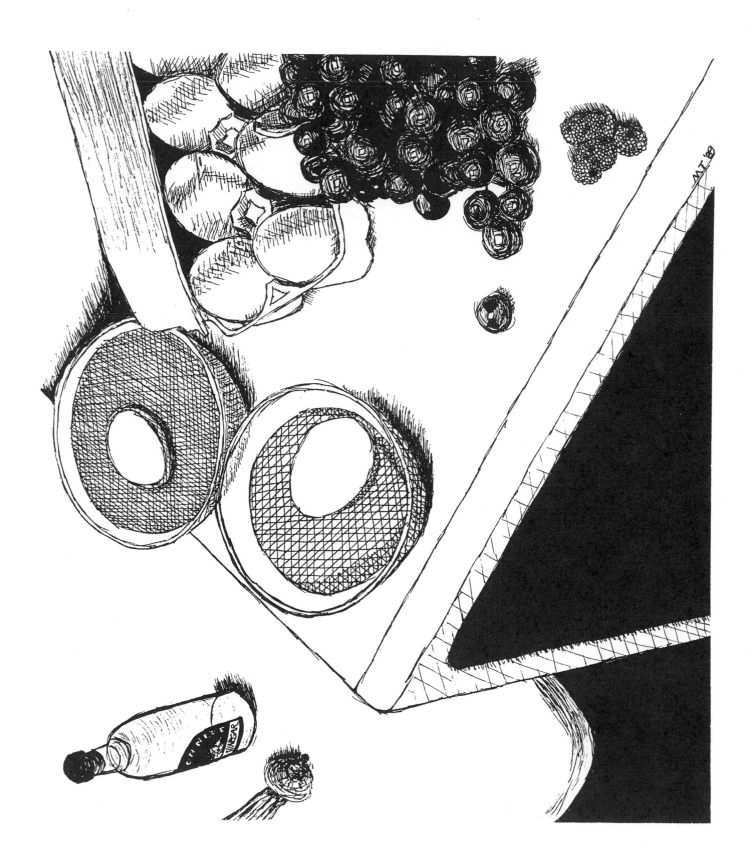

# NATURE CRAFTS

The great outdoors is a wonderful place to collect items for crafts projects. By using natural items, children learn about the world around them. Many children enjoy going on neighborhood walks or field trips to collect these materials. It is important to teach children to be respectful of nature; pick wild flowers only where they grow abundantly. Never take more than 10% of a clump or pull them up by their roots. Tread gently so the ecology is not disrupted and leave an area as neat as you found it. Take cones, twigs, pods, and leaves from the ground whenever possible, rather than pulling them off the trees. Never pull whole branches or stalks off of plants or trees. Pinch leaves off gently and take from a wide range of the plant rather than just off one branch. Be sure to teach children why it is important to be respectful of nature.

Several of the nature crafts projects involve using food such as fruits, vegetables and seeds. Some people feel that the use of food is inappropriate for crafts projects because there is so much hunger in the world. Please use your own judgment and discretion.

# NATURE CRAFTS

## SAND CASTING WITH PLASTER

*MATERIALS NEEDED:* Plaster of Paris, a coffee can, damp sand, rocks, shells, drift wood, beach glass, and other interestingly shaped objects.

*SET-UP:*

1. This project can be done at the beach or at school. If at school put wet sand in a shallow box. If at the beach, the mold can be made right in the sand.

2. Collect the rocks, shells and other items.

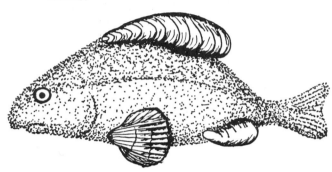

*PROCEDURE:*

1. Make a mold by scooping out the wet sand. Leave at least two inches of sand covering the bottom of the box. For a fish shape make the mold 6 inches wide, 12 inches long and 2 inches deep. For a fossil the mold can be round in shape. Other possibilities include: an impression of a shell, a child's hand or foot, or a free-form pattern.

2. Press the shells, rocks and other found items into the bottom of the mold. Holes can be poked into the sand for indentations.

3. Mix the plaster in the coffee can according to the directions on the box.

4. Stir the plaster with hands or an old long spoon.

5. Wait five minutes and then pour the plaster carefully into the mold.

6. Let the sand cast harden for at least one hour and lift it out of the sand.

7. Brush off the loose sand.

*COMMENTS:*

Plaster of Paris should not be poured down a drain and can not be washed out of containers. It hardens very quickly, so do not mix it in advance.

## PAINTED-ROCKS

*MATERIALS NEEDED:* Rocks of all shapes and sizes (smooth ones and round ones work best), acrylic paints, glue, yarn, shells, wiggle eyes, pipe cleaners, cardboard, and felt.

*SET-UP:*

1. Collect rocks and pebbles.

2. Clean and dry the rocks before painting.

3. Cut cardboard bases for the rock creations if desired.

*PROCEDURE:*

1. Children glue rocks together to create dolls, people, animals, monsters, etc. They may also wish to glue rocks together to make free-form rock sculptures.

2. Glue smaller rocks onto the larger ones for the head, arms and legs.

3. Paint faces, clothing, designs, etc.

4. Yarn and felt can be added for hair and clothing. Wiggle eyes and pipe cleaners can be used to create bugs or monsters.

5. Small shells can be glued on for decoration.

**128**

Shoe boxes, egg cartons or other containers can be decorated to hold or display the painted rocks.

## DRIFTWOOD SCULPTURE

*MATERIALS NEEDED:* Driftwood pieces, small shells and rocks, glue.

*SET-UP:*

1. Collect the driftwood pieces, shells and rocks.

2. Ask the children to find the most interesting pieces of driftwood they can.

*PROCEDURE:*

1. Children put pieces of driftwood together to create sculptures. They can make animals, people or free form shapes.

2. Glue on shells, rocks or any other object needed to achieve their effect.

*COMMENTS:*

Driftwood, shells and small rocks can also be made into mobiles. Use twigs with string to support the nature items.

## LEAF DECORATIONS ON CARDS AND STATIONERY

*MATERIALS NEEDED:* Colorful leaves (of all shapes, sizes and varieties), newspaper, glue and heavy weight paper, large index cards or cardboard.

*SET-UP:*

1. Collect the leaves with the children.

*PROCEDURE:*

1. Press the leaves between pieces of newspaper by placing a heavy book or object on top of them until they dry. This will take several days.

2. For stationery, cut paper into several pieces of the same size .

3. Then carefully glue a leaf or some leaves on the top of the paper. Or glue onto light cardboard or index cards to make greeting cards.

## FLOWER PAINTING

*MATERIALS NEEDED:* colorful flowers and weeds, and paper

*SET-UP:*

1. Collect flowers in your neighborhood such as dandelions, goldenrod, wild aster and/or any other colorful flowering plant. Also ask your local floral shop to donate old flowers such as roses, carnations, etc.

*PROCEDURE:*

1. Children simply use the flower heads and rub them on the paper.

2. For large flowers, several petals can be rolled into a ball and then used. The color pigment of the flowers will transfer onto the paper.

*COMMENTS:*

Many younger children will be fascinated by seeing the color pigment transfer onto the paper. For older children it is a good comparison study of different flower colors.

## NATURAL PAINTS

*MATERIALS NEEDED:* A variety of items such as parsley, black tea, grape skins, red cabbage, beets, pear leaves, cherry leaves, blueberries, flower petals, oak bark, and green leaves, a sauce pan, a burner, water, paint brushes, light colored paper and containers for paint.

*SET-UP:*

1. Collect the plants and items that will be used for the paint.

2. Show the children examples of natural dyes.

*PROCEDURE:*

1. Separately chop or shred small pieces of the plant materials.

2. Put them one at a time in a sauce pan with a very small amount of water (just enough to prevent burning) and simmer until the water turns colorful.

3. Pour the colored water into paint containers and let cool.

4. Paint on a light colored paper with brushes.

## PAINTING WITH NATURE

*MATERIALS NEEDED:* Paper, large containers for paint, and paint. A choice of corn cobs with or without corn; a pineapple; pine needle clusters; a pine cone; cattails; leafy tops of vegetables such as beets, celery, parsnips, radishes, turnips or carrots.

*SET-UP.*

1. Collect the item(s) that will be used for painting.

2. Set out paint in shallow dishes and paper.

*PROCEDURE:*

1. Dip the "brushes" into paint and simply paint with them.

2. Corncobs, pineapples (cut off the leaves) and pine cones should be rolled into paint and evenly coated, then rolled across the paper.

## AIR DRYING FLOWERS

*MATERIALS NEEDED:* Flowers, a wire coat hanger, rubber bands, string, long pipe cleaners, a shoe box, a nail, and waterproofing spray.

*SET-UP:*

1. Pick the flowers on a sunny day when they are in full bloom and make sure they are not wet with dew. The best time to pick flowers is in the morning.

2. Cut the stems as long as possible and on a slant.

*PROCEDURE:*

1. To prepare the flowers for drying, pull all the leaves off the stem.

2. Bunch flowers together, put only three together if the flower is large; put up to six together for smaller flowers.

3. Twist one end of a long pipe cleaner tightly around the stems of a bunch of flowers.

4. Twist the other end of the pipe cleaner over the wire rod of the hanger and hang four to six bunches of flowers upside-down (see diagram).

5. Suspend the hangers in a warm, dry, dark room, garage or basement.

6. Let dry two to three weeks (the larger the flower, the longer it will take to dry). The stems will shrink and become stiff.

7. To preserve the flowers, spray with waterproofing.

*COMMENTS:*

Dried flowers can be used for a variety of crafts projects. They look beautiful in homemade vases, wall hangings, weaving, and baskets. Carpentry projects can be enhanced with dried flowers. Seed pods and natural materials such as berries can also be air dried. Some flowers will wilt and shrink when air-dried. There are books that list which flowers work best, or you can experiment with many flowers to see which work well.

## OLD-FASHIONED FLOWER PRESSING

*MATERIALS NEEDED:* Small flat flowers such as pansy, phlox or primrose, ink blotter or smooth paper towel, and heavy books (dictionary or big city telephone book).

*SET-UP:*

1. Pick the flowers on a hot sunny day and make sure they are dry. Check with your local Parks and Recreation division to find out if there are areas where flower picking is permitted. Also ask neighborhood garden owners if some flowers can be picked. If there is no place to pick fresh flowers, purchase them.

2. Cut off the stems at the base of the flower; save some for pressing.

3. The flowers can be picked at different stages of growth.

*PROCEDURE:*

1. Open each of the books about 1/2 inch from the back cover. Lay the blotter or paper towel on the right side of the page (see diagram).

2. Place freshly picked flowers face down on the blotter and press down the center of the flower with your index finger.

3. When the blotter is filled with flowers, cover it with another blotter or paper towel. For additional flowers, turn down another 1/2 inch thickness of pages and press the flowers as above.

4. Close the book when all the flowers are in between the pages. To press the flowers, put several heavy books on top of the book with the flowers inside.

5. Place in a dry, warm place and let sit for at least two weeks.

6. Dried flowers will have hard stiff centers and petals that feel brittle.

## MODERN FLOWER PRESSING

*MATERIALS NEEDED:* Flowers, silica gel (sodium silicate which can be purchased from a drugstore, a flower shop or craft shop), a large box and large plastic bag.

*SET-UP:*

1. See Old-Fashioned Flower Pressing for picking and preparation of flowers.

2. Cut two pieces of blotter paper to fit inside of the box.

*PROCEDURE:*

1. Place one piece of blotter paper in the box and cover with 1/4 inch of silica gel. The gel preserves the flowers natural color and absorbs wetness.

2. Put the flowers on top of the silica gel in a single layer leaving space between the flowers.

3. Cover the flowers with another 1/4 inch layer of silica gel and then with the second piece of blotter paper.

4. Put a heavy book on top of the box; then carefully place the box with the book into a plastic bag. Tightly close the bag.

5. Place several more books on top of the plastic bag.

6. Keep on a level surface in a dry, warm room.

7. Let dry two to three days.

*COMMENTS:*

If the petals are not smooth, place the flowers back inside a book for a few more days without the blotter or gel. Pressed flowers make wonderful crafts projects. They can be glued onto paper for stationery, pressed into clay, or used to make pictures and decorate windows.

## OLD-FASHIONED VEGETABLE EGG DYING

*MATERIALS NEEDED:* Hard-boiled eggs, cheesecloth or clean old nylons, a twist tie, vinegar, scissors, a small pan, a burner and the following materials for dyes:

> *Blue* - red cabbage leaves or blueberries
>
> *Pink* - rose hips, cherries or pickled beet juice
>
> *Bluish purple* - diced beets
>
> *Pale green* - spinach leaves, young grass, broccoli, or carrot tops
>
> *Bright yellow* - saffron tea
>
> *Pale yellow* -yellow onion skins, dandelion, or goldenrod flowers

*Dark brown* - red and brown onion skins

*Light brown* - walnut shells

*Brown* - coffee or tea

*Purple* - grape juice

*Orange* - grated carrots

*SET-UP:*

1. Purchase the vegetables.

2. Cut the cheesecloth or nylons into 4"x 4" pieces.

3. Hard boil the eggs.

*PROCEDURE:*

1. Chop a vegetable up into small pieces.

2. Put 3 tablespoons of the chopped vegetable matter in the center of the material.

3. Center the egg in the piece of material and spread the vegetable chunks around it evenly.

4. Secure the material around the egg with a twist tie.

5. Place the wrapped egg in a small pan, cover with water so there is about 1/2" of water over the egg.

6. Bring to a boil and simmer for about ten minutes.

7. Let the egg cool in the water.

8. Add one teaspoon of vinegar.

COMMENTS:

This is a long process, and you will need new water and vinegar for each egg and color. This project produces eggs with patterns around them. The eggs can be eaten after the dying process.

## NATURAL EGG-DYING

MATERIALS NEEDED: Hard boiled, raw or blown eggs, salt (raw eggs only), vinegar, a pot, and a burner. Use the same materials for dyes as found in Old-Fashioned Vegetable Egg Dying.

SET-UP:

1. Simmer all ingredients separately, except the pickled beet juice and the grape juice.

PROCEDURE:

1. Talk to the children about the use of natural dyes in clothing, paintings, pottery, and painting.

2. Dye some eggs and see if the children can guess what materials were used to make the color.

3. Simmer eggs with one of the ingredients mentioned above.

4. For the pink dye, soak hard boiled eggs in pickled beet juice.

5. To dye the eggs a lavender shade soak them in grape juice.

6. If raw eggs are used, put several onto a pan with a pinch of salt. Add a large handful of dying material and bring to a boil. Immediately reduce the heat and simmer the eggs for 12 minutes. This method produces a richer, brighter dye color. Cool with 1 t. vinegar added to water before removing.

COMMENTS:

This project produces solid colored eggs. Dying eggs naturally is very educational! However, it is time-consuming. The easiest way to color eggs is with commercial food coloring (liquid or tablets). White crayons drawn on the eggs before dying will result in a resist-type design. Other colored crayons can be used to create patterns between the dye. Eggs can be dipped into more than one color. Hand-painting is also a fun activity. Another variation is wrapping yarn around eggs. The eggs can be eaten after the dying process.

## OAK LEAF EGG-DYING

MATERIALS NEEDED: Fresh oak leaves, eggs, rubber bands or string, and a pot and burner.

SET-UP:

1. Collect fresh oak leaves.

2. Hard-boil the eggs.

3. Set the leaves and other materials on art table.

PROCEDURE:

1. Wrap oak leaves around an egg and fasten securely with rubber bands or string..

2. Simmer several eggs for seven to ten minutes.

3. Remove the eggs from the pot and let cool.

4. Gently peel the leaves off. The leaves will make a dappled brownish effect on the eggs.

COMMENTS:

The eggs can be eaten after they have been dyed.

## SEED DECORATIONS

*MATERIALS NEEDED:* Seeds of all shapes, colors, sizes and textures, varnish (optional), glue, and items to be decorated with seeds such as burlap, cork board, felt, a blown egg, cardboard, a glass jar, a tin, and plastic containers.

*SET-UP:* Collect or purchase seeds. Have children bring in dried fruit and vegetable seeds. On nature walks collect, flower heads, fir cones, acorns, sycamore and ash wings and other seeds . Corn and other seeds can be purchased at pet shops. Look for wheat, maple, sesame seeds, peas, sunflower seeds, bird food, gold sweetcorn, black eyed peas, millet, Chinese and European lentils, brown, red, white, soya, pale green flageolet, and black beans at local grocery stores, international food and health food shops.

*PROCEDURE:*

1. Seeds can be used to decorate a variety of items. For a simple design have children draw a picture on cardboard and fill it in with seeds. For a more complex project seeds can be used to decorate bottles, cardboard boxes, jars, and cans. Wall hangings can be made on cloth, burlap, and felt. Use a strong piece of cardboard for the backing and frames. Cork board and wooden panels can be decorated with seeds without any backing. Blown eggshells can be decorated with seeds and hung from a tree or window.

2. To glue the seeds, it is best to begin with a simple design using middle-sized and larger seeds. Younger children should put the glue down first and then carefully place each seed on top of the glue. Older children may use a toothpick or a small paint brush to apply the glue to the back of each seed. Smaller seeds create more elaborate designs but are difficult to use. Shells can be included in the designs for variation.

3. Let the seeds dry before applying varnish. Glue mixed with water can also be applied. The varnish will increase the richness of the color and will protect the seeds from dust. It also will help keep the small seeds in place. If the design is made on fabric or glass, the varnish must be brushed on very carefully to avoid touching the background. Spray varnish can also be used on painted backgrounds.

# PLANTING AND GROWING

Spring is a fabulous time to do planting and growing activities with children. If you are fortunate enough to have an outside garden, children can learn the process of plant growth first hand. Even if you do not have an outside garden, there are many different gardening projects that can be done. Everything from growing mold to planting indoor bulbs to caring for hanging plants provides children with interesting hands-on experiences with plant life. Allowing the children to take responsibility for the proper care of the plants enhances their experiences.

## IDEAS FOR PLANTING AND GROWING PROJECTS:

### FRUITS AND VEGETABLE GARDENS

Why not try growing:

| | | |
|---|---|---|
| avocado pits | potatoes | pineapple tops |
| carrot tops | fruit seeds | bulbs |
| pop corn kernels | peanuts | beans |

### PLANTING AND GROWING EXPERIMENTS

Try science experiments when introducing planting and growing.

**1.** Purchase three identical plants. Put one in a very sunny place, one in a partly sunny place and place one in the shade. Care for each plant the same. Have children note the progress of each plant.

**2.** Plant several of the same seeds in different types of soil. See which one is the most healthy and thriving.

**3.** Purchase different types of plant food and see which is most effective.

**4.** Try a variety of ways to sprout seeds such as cotton balls sitting in jars with water, in soil, and in jars of water. Which works best?

# PLANTING AND GROWING

## POTATO CREATURES

*MATERIALS NEEDED:* Potatoes, potting soil, grass seeds, a knife, a spoon, marking pens, tooth picks; and for decorations — raisins, small marshmallows, buttons, material, etc.

*SET-UP:*

1. Bring in potatoes with no sprouted eyes.

2. Make sure you have a sunny window sill or table on which to place the potatoes.

*PROCEDURE:*

1. Cut the potatoes in half either lengthwise or vertically.

2. Scoop out the insides of the potatoes.

3. Fill the insides with potting soil.

4. Plant the grass seeds inside.

5. Use tooth picks for legs.

6. Draw a face on the potato with a marking pen and decorate.

7. Small pieces of potato can be cut for ears and tails and secured with tooth picks.

8. Put in a sunny place and keep moist.

*COMMENTS:*

Monsters, bunnies, cats, people, and other creatures can be created. Send them home as soon as the grass has grown a few inches because the potatoes will start to rot after a week or so. Some people feel that the use of food is inappropriate for crafts projects because there is so much hunger in the world. Please use your own judgment and discretion. Other containers can be substituted for the potatoes such as egg cartons, milk cartons, or margarine tubs.

## MINI GARDENS

*MATERIALS NEEDED:* A variety of seeds in packages, egg cartons, potting soil, small rocks, tooth picks, paper clips, and masking tape.

*SET-UP:*

1. This project is best done outdoors, or with newspaper covering the art table.

2. Open the seed packages, making sure not to rip the name.

3. Put out the above materials for each child.

*PROCEDURE:*

1. Sprinkle a small layer of rocks into each cup of the egg carton, for drainage.

2. Fill each egg cup 3/4 full with potting soil.

3. Push fingers into the soil to make holes for the seeds.

4. Plant two or three seeds in each of the twelve egg cups (follow the directions on each package), and cover with soil.

5. Label the seeds by making mini-signs (masking tape folded over a tooth pick).

6. Bring the gardens indoors, put them in a sunny place, and water them daily.

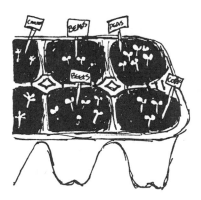

*COMMENTS:*

Plastic plant containers with holes in the bottom also work well for mini gardens. Plants can be replanted in gardens or large pots.

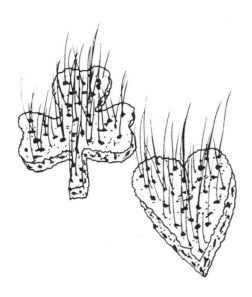

## HAIRY SPONGES

*MATERIALS NEEDED:* Sponges, a marking pen, sharp scissors, fast growing seeds such as grass, a pie tin or shallow dish, and plenty of sunshine.

*SET-UP:*

1. Make sure you have a window sill or table that receives ample sunlight.

*PROCEDURE:*

1. Draw a shape or object on the sponge.

2. Cut out the shape.

3. Wet the sponge shape.

4. Place the sponge shape in the shallow dish of water.

5. Press the seeds into the holes of the sponge.

6. Put in a sunny place.

7. Keep moist.

*COMMENTS:*

The seeds will grow out of the sponge shape. This is a great project for St. Patrick's Day. Cut the sponges into shamrocks and plant grass seeds. Pop-up sponge sheets can be purchased that expand when placed in water. (See Sponge Painting in the Painting Section for more information).

## HANGING SPONGE GARDENS

*MATERIALS NEEDED:* small sponges, clear plastic bags, fast growing seeds (grass, clover, mustard, chia or herbs), and strings.

*SET-UP:*

1. The gardens need to be suspended in a sunny spot.

*PROCEDURE:*

1. Moisten the sponges.

2. Push the seeds into the holes of the top side of the sponge.

3. Carefully place the sponge inside a plastic bag with the seeds facing upwards.

4. Tie the string around the top of the bag and suspend in a sunny spot.

5. Watch the seeds germinate inside the bag!

6. Keep moist. They can be transplanted but many will not survive.

## SPROUTS

*MATERIALS NEEDED:* Alfalfa seeds, mung beans, lentils, soy beans or other edible legumes and seeds; small clean window screen(s) covered with light weight porous fabric (i.e. muslin, gauze); jar(s) to soak seeds, area to drain the screen easily.

*SET UP:*

1. If a regular window screen is available, just measure and cut the fabric to fit on it, and another piece to go over the top so light does not get directly on the screen.

2. Screens can be made with hardware store screening material, wooden frames and staples and small nails.

3. Test the fabric to make sure water will drain through it easily, before using it on the screens.

*PROCEDURE:*

1. Soak a handful of the seeds or beans in the jar for several hours, up to eight, but not longer. How many seeds used will depend on the size of the screen and the type of seeds or bean. The seeds will need to have room to grow.

2. Drain the water from the seeds or beans, and spread them out evenly on the fabric covering the screen. Put another layer of the fabric over the seeds or beans. Set in a shady spot that is not too cold.

3. For the next few days, water the seeds on the screen twice a day. This is done by lightly spraying water over the seeds directly, and allowing the water to drain off immediately. (Doing this over lawn or some other water loving vegetation is best to conserve water use). Re-cover the seeds each time they are watered.

4. Make sure that the seeds do not sit in any water while on the screen, and if the watering process causes them to clump together, lightly spread them out again by hand.

5. After three or four days, the seeds or beans will be ready to harvest. Legumes will take longer than smaller seeds, alfalfa is the fastest growing. Uncover the tray and expose the sprouts to sunlight for several hours, 4 to 12. The leaves will turn green.

6. Now eat them for snack. Try different types for a taste experience. Cooking the legume sprouts is also a taste treat mixed with rice or noodles. Wheat sprouts are very sweet and can be added to bread, however, they should be harvested without the sunlight exposure.

*COMMENTS:*

Purchasing some sprouts at the grocery store will show children what they can expect to see, and also give the teacher an idea of what the seeds and beans should look like when they are ready. Seeds will grow at different rates depending on type, temperature and light around them, and amounts of water. Drainage is very important. If the weather is very warm, water the seeds a third time each day. Adults should try the whole cycle in advance at home, to insure that the seeds are viable, the soaking time works, and to determine how long each type of seed takes in their climate.

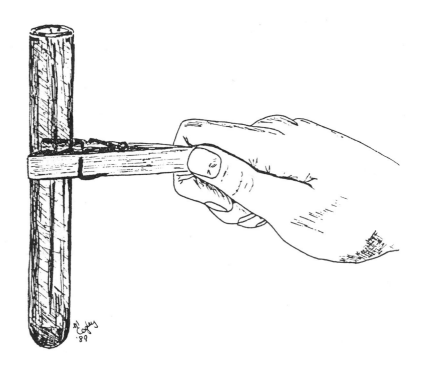

# Diagram of bulbs

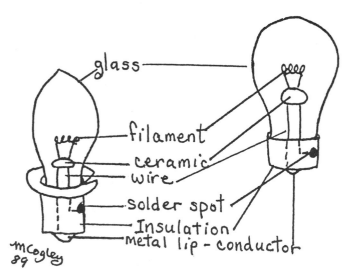

glass

filament

ceramic

wire

solder spot

Insulation

metal lip - conductor

# SCIENCE

Some public schools have ongoing integrated science programs in the classrooms; many do not. After school programs have the opportunity to offer hands-on and exciting science programs. It is common for teachers to be initially uncomfortable with the idea of presenting science, other than nature study. However, when children observe the natural occurrences around them, they are beginning their science awareness.

Many after school programs have a table set up for nature-type items. These tables may contain bugs, small animals, leaves, rocks, and shells. This is an excellent idea and themes can be expanded to include things such as crystals, magnets, mold, optical illusions, magnifying glasses, microscopes, seasonal objects and pictures, snakes, space, environments (like deserts or forests), and plants and sprouts. The items on the table should change regularly (about every 2-3 weeks) and be set up to allow touching whenever reasonable. A background of posters or National Geographic pictures is an excellent addition to this area. There are impressive nature study books available with wonderful ideas for a table or corner. A science table helps the children focus on science that is everywhere around them, and helps teach observation skills. The items and pictures lead the children to notice, explore, and question; which are vital ingredients in any science program.

However, this type of table area should not be all there is to a science program. Science is also the process of finding answers, by making, observing, experimenting and researching. Adults often feel uneasy presenting the more technical areas of scientific inquiry, and this is reflected in their science offerings. It is necessary for children to explore things like batteries, wires, chemicals, and parts of appliances. They need hands-on experiments and opportunities to deviate from the standard texts if the process of exploration takes them that way.

Science On A Shoe String is a very fine collection of science projects and experiments that can be set up easily and inexpensively. The book itself is an asset to a program. They also sell sets containing all the materials needed: however, many of the same materials can be found inexpensively at variety and grocery stores. Jerald Tunheim and Judy Branum from Dakota State College and South Dakota State University have worked together to develop an exciting program of physics experiments for children. They present their ideas at workshops and have developed Science and Physics Education for Early Childhood Teachers and Their Young Children. Their program includes a manual and an optional kit. Their projects are geared towards older grades as well as younger, and for science enthusiasts as well as novices. These sources along with many other books with good science projects and experiments are listed in the Reference Section at the end of the book.

# SUGGESTIONS FOR SCIENCE PROJECTS

**1.** Do science projects in small groups of 10 children or less.

**2.** Allow each group to experiment at least once every week to two weeks.

**3.** Promote questioning and exploring.

**4.** Make your experiments as hands-on as possible.

**5.** Do an activity in advance so you know what to expect.

**6.** Allow children to deviate.

**7.** Stress observation skills as a scientific tool.


Some good ways to start experimenting:

1. Find appliances that are no longer working such as calculators, T.V.'s, radios, and battery operated toys. Remove the electrical cords prior to investigating. Have the children dismantle them. Provide pliers and different size phillips and flathead screwdrivers. Battery-operated toys have little motors in them that are great to discover and watch turn, after they have been dissected from the toy. *Caution:* be sure to remove the batteries and check for battery acid in the toys.

2. Put an "Experimentation table" outside. Set the following items and utensils in containers, on the table. Provide empty containers for combining them.

　　1. Mix vinegar and baking soda, or oil and water.

　　2. Stir and blow food coloring and soap with straws.

　　3. Put out colored water, vinegar, and oil to see what mixes, sinks or floats.

　　4. Set up straws, funnels, and measuring cups or rulers, tape and items to measure, to see relationships.

3. Allow the children to just "play" with the items on the table.

4. Help steer their focus into observing and commenting on what is happening when things are combined. Ask questions that allow for discussion or further observation such as:

　　1. What is happening to the baking soda?

　　2. Where do you think the tiny bubbles are coming from?

　　3. What do you see?

　　4. What do they do when you mix them?

　　5. Can you find something else that does the same thing?

**RAIN MAKING**

*PURPOSE:* To observe change from liquid to gas, and back again.

*MATERIALS:* A cookie sheet; a sauce pan or tea kettle; a heat source; another pan or pot to catch the "rain"; optional: a drawing of the rain cycle (see diagram).

*GRADES:* K - 6

*SET-UP:*

1. Fill sauce pan or tea kettle with water.

2. Discuss with the children how some things change when heat is applied. Can they think of things that do? (baked goods, snow water).

3. Remind them that *observation* is the key to science.

*PROCEDURE:*

1. Heat the pot or pan until the water is slowly boiling.

2. Hold the cookie sheet over the water high enough so the steam can rise and form drops on the bottom. Ask them what is happening now?

3. As the steam condenses, it will begin to fall off the cookie sheet and land on the object you have strategically placed beneath where it will fall.

4. Add ice to the pot and start over. What happens? Does it take longer? Does it work?

5. Show them the rain cycle drawing and discuss how the experiment follows the same plan — heating, evaporating, condensing, and falling.

*COMMENTS:*

This simple experiment is primarily teacher-directed, and stresses observation skills. Promote discussion throughout it to increase the group's involvement. Slightly tilting the cookie sheet will help the "rain" fall where you want it to land.

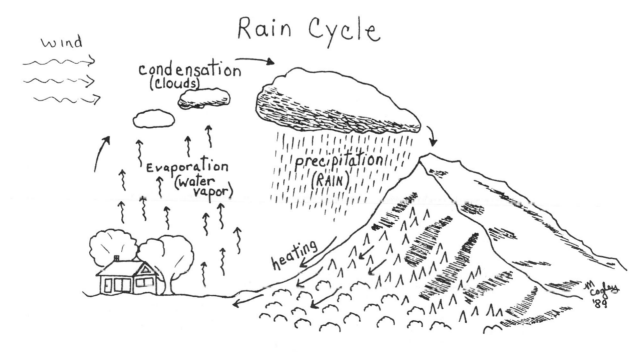

Rain Cycle

## COLORED DROPS

*PURPOSE:* To develop observation skills.

*MATERIALS NEEDED:* Red and green food coloring, eye droppers, liquid water softener, waxed paper, pencils, and water.

*GRADES:* 2 - 6

*SET UP:*

1. Before beginning, mix red food coloring and a small amount of water together, to make bright red. Then mix green food coloring and water together with one or two drops of water softener. Have this ready before the children sit down. The red should drop onto waxed paper in a firm dome, the green should fall flat and run.

2. Divide the children into groups of two. Provide each group with three 6" X 6" pieces of waxed paper and two pencils.

*PROCEDURE:*

1. Give each team half an eye-dropper of the red mixture. Allow them to roll it, touch it with the pencils and/or their fingers, wiggle the paper, and smell it. Ask for comments.

2. Put the waxed paper with the red aside for a few minutes, and give them the same amount of green mix. Allow time for observation and comments. How does this compare to the red? Have the children put a little of the green onto a red drop. What happens? (The red will flatten out right away).

3. Ask the children to predict which mixture acts most like regular water.

4. Give them half a dropper of regular water on the third waxed paper sheet. (It acts like red mix). Give time to observe and compare.

5. Allow time for investigating, or to try the experiment on other types of surfaces. Discuss what happened and explain the difference in how the mixes were made. Ask the children what they think water softener does, how water acts differently on waxed and unwaxed paper, what the waxed paper is good for, and how water softener helps.

*COMMENTS:*

The water softener breaks up the surface tension of the water and flattens it.

## LIQUIDS, SOLIDS, AND GASES

*PURPOSE:* Classification by property

*MATERIALS NEEDED:* Three plastic baggies per student, twist ties to close them, pencils, and solid and liquid substances.

*GRADES:* K - 4

*SET-UP:*

1. Take one baggie and fill it with a solid material (i.e. a rock), another with water, and leave the third for later.

2. Have the children sit in a circle and talk with you for a few minutes.

*PROCEDURE:*

1. Show the solid baggie and have the children describe it. Demonstrate the properties.

    Properties of solids are:

    1. do not change shape easily

    2. are usually visible

    3. another solid cannot easily pass through it

2. Show the liquid baggie and have them describe it. Add a little food coloring to help them see movement.

    Properties of liquids are:

    1. change shape easily

    2. can be visible or invisible

    3. solids can pass through it easily (show this)

3. Show them the third empty baggie. What is in it? (Nothing). Blow into it. What is in it now? (Air). Air is a gas. Can you see it, does it change shapes? Open the bag and describe it with their help.

Properties of gases are:

1. Change shape easily

2. Usually invisible (polluted air is not)

3. Solids pass through easily

4. Let the children collect their own substances. Have them show their bags and tell why they have classified them as liquid, solid or gas.

5. Make a long list of possible liquids, gases and solids. (Watch out for glass, and for silly putty; those are tricky to classify.)

## ALKA-SELTZER TESTING

*PURPOSE:* Observation of properties

*MATERIALS:* For every two children: one Alka-Seltzer tablet, 2 clear plastic cups (or other container), hand magnifying glass, matches or a candle, small paper (white and dark colored), pencils, water, one glass test tube, spoons (optional). For the teacher, a large sheet of paper and marking pen or chalk board.

*GRADES:* 3 - 5

*SET-UP:*

1. Divide the children into pairs, and pass out the materials.

2. Have the children fill a plastic cup, one third full of water, in preparation for experimentation, and have it at their place.

*PROCEDURE:*

1. Tell the children they are going to investigate the properties of the Alka-Seltzer. Caution the children that these are medicine and not to be eaten. Place the unused tablets well out of reach.

2. Write the possible properties on the board or a large sheet of paper. (Properties means the important characteristics of any substance, i.e. color, weight {density}, hardness, smell, feel, taste, does it dissolve?, etc.)

3. Ask the children to break the tablet into four sections.

4. Take a quarter tablet and crush it onto a piece of dark paper with fingers or a spoon. Look at the crushed pieces with the magnifying glass. Notice the differences in the shapes and sizes of the pieces. Have them draw what they see (powder and crystals ).

5. Next, put a quarter tablet into the test tube and fill it one fourth full of water. Have the children put their fingers over the top and feel what is escaping, (gas). Also have them feel the bottom of the tube. (It will feel cold because heat energy is required to help the reaction occur and the water cools as the tablet dissolves).

6. Put a quarter tablet into a cup and cover it just barely with water. Light the match and hold it over the escaping gas without touching the water. What happens to the flame? (Carbon dioxide is created by the dissolving tablet, the $CO_2$ escapes, and puts out the flame). Repeat this after a few minutes with the same cup. Now what happens to the flame? (The $CO_2$ is gone, and the match burns). (The candle provides a somewhat safer flame for this part, but the wax tends to drip into the seltzer).

7. Let the children play with and investigate the last quarter tablet on their own. Tell them they can taste it if they want. Tell them to write down what they notice.

8. Discuss the experiments as a group and write properties they observed on the paper or board. What worked? What did not?

*COMMENTS:*

For variation, try different types of Alka Seltzer.

## SOAP PLANT

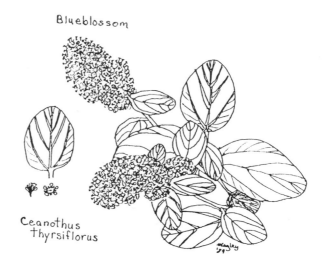

Blueblossom

Ceanothus
thyrsiflorus

*PURPOSE:* To demonstrate
natural uses for plants, and integrate concepts from both Social Studies and Science.

*MATERIALS:* Blueblossom
(*Ceanothus Thyrsiflorus* — see
illustration), water, towels,
several bowls.

*GRADES:* K - 6

*SET-UP:*

1. If you want to compare the dried
blossoms with the fresh, you will need
to pick at least one stalk per child
about a week ahead of time. When
gathering the blossoms, pinch or cut
the plant carefully at the end of the
flower head. Pick the same quantity of
fresh blossoms for each child, plus a
couple extra.

2. To dry, lay the blossoms out on a
clean, dry surface. Be sure they are not
touching each other. When dry (about
5 days), strip all the flowers off the
stems and put them back out to dry for
another 2 days.

3. Put bowls, towels and pitchers of
water on a table or other large flat surface. If there are not many children,
you can use a sink instead. Doing it on
a table allows large groups to do this
project.

4. Divide the children into groups
depending on how many bowls you
have. There should be two for each
group. One with warm water, one with
cold. Provide a bucket of rinse water
set to the side for getting all the blossoms off of the children's hands.

*PROCEDURE:*

1. Discuss the fact that early people on
all continents including Native
Americans used wild plants for different uses. Give the children some
ideas, and see if they can figure some
out. Tell the name of the plant you are
going to use, common and technical.

2. Demonstrate by dipping your hands

in water, then rubbing a fresh blossom
head briskly between both hands. If there
are no suds, use more water and rub harder. These blossoms really suds up!

3. Look at the fresh blossoms and the
dried ones and have children comment on
the differences. Hypothesize which will
suds better. Take a prediction vote and
write results down for later comparison.

4. The children should each have a chance
to try fresh and dried blossoms, and warm
and cold water.

5. Have the group discuss their observations. What happened? Which combination worked best? Why was the cold water
important? (In past history people often
bathed in the streams and rivers). Is this
soap ecological? Why were the dried blossoms important? (During the winter
months when there were no fresh available).

*COMMENTS:*

Ceanothus has shiny green leaves and
clusters of blossoms, either white or
bluish. It is often used as a landscape
decoration and is, therefore, fairly easily
found. Ask the property owner, or park officials first, and they may allow you to
return every year. This project can be the
beginning of integrating Science and Social Studies, or a study of the Native
Americans, State History, or an introduction to Ecology. Many other members of
the Ceanothus family were used all across
the United States. Amole soap root is
another excellent sudsy plant, but much
less accessible in large quantities.

## CHEMICAL GARDENS

*PURPOSE:* To observe changes.

*MATERIALS:* Laundry bluing (caution, this stains certain materials), water, salt, ammonia (caution, avoid inhalation and if skin comes in contact with the ammonia, carefully rinse the skin with water), charcoal, pieces of old bricks, rocks, sponges, foil or glass pie tins, food coloring, some measuring cups, and empty containers.

*GRADES:* 3 - 5

*SET-UP:*

1. Divide the children into groups of 3 or 4.

2. Give each group several rocks, sponges, pieces of charcoal and bricks, three pie tins or plates, and an empty container.

3. Put the bluing, ammonia, water, salt, and measuring cups in a central, easily monitored spot. This area should be well supervised.

*PROCEDURE:*

1. Have each group arrange their pie tins with charcoal, bricks, or rocks. Some groups may want to have one tin with only charcoal, one with only brick, etc., others may want a variety. Allow freedom to mix and match.

2. An adult should be present during all pouring and mixing. A representative from each group goes to the "mixing area". They put 1/4 cup ammonia, 1/4 cup salt, 1/4 cup bluing, and 1/4 cup warm water together into their empty container. (A quarter cup is 4 Tablespoons).

3. The mixture is poured over the tins evenly.

4. Another representative gets the food coloring and drops a few drops onto each piece of rock, brick, sponge, or charcoal.

5. Put the tins in a safe spot to sit overnight. In the next day or so they will be covered with what looks like colored moss.

6. Have the children observe which substance has the most "moss" and which grows the fastest? slowest? Which does not grow well? Discuss possible reasons why or why not. (The "moss" is the solidification of the chemicals in combination).

*COMMENTS:*

Charcoal will absorb more mixture than the bricks, and the rocks will not absorb much at all, unless you use a sandstone type. Try this with other things as bases; shells, tiles, terracotta, pottery shards.

## CORN POPPING

*PURPOSE:* To note that heat can change things; corn contains moisture.

*MATERIALS:* Popcorn kernels, matches, cooking oil, several eye droppers, one test tube for every two children, one clothes pin per test tube, small pieces of aluminum foil (one 2"X 2", another 4" X 4") for each pair, one candle per pair.

*GRADES:* K - 6

*SET-UP:*

1. Set several eye droppers and a container of oil to one side.

2. Tell the children they are going to observe changes made by heat.

3. Explain safety rules for using candles.

4. Pass out materials; give each pair of children a test tube, matches, one piece of both sizes of foil, three or four kernels of corn, one clothes pin, and one candle.

5. Demonstrate how to attach the clothes pin onto the tube, or have it already done for them, (see diagram). Also state that test tubes should never be pointed toward anyone.

*PROCEDURE:*

1. Ask the children if the corn is moist or dry; take a vote.

2. Show them how to fold the small foil piece to make a cover for the tube. Set it to one side for a while.

3. Light the candle and drip some wax onto the large foil piece. Set the candle into the melted wax until it firms. This will hold the candle steady during the experiment.

4. Have one team member put a drop of oil into the tube.

5. Put one corn kernel into the tube and put the foil cover over the top. Put the tube over the flame, but keep it

one inch above the flame. (If the tube gets into the flame, it will turn black but can be wiped off when cool).

6. With the clothes pin, hold the test tube over the flame, and move it gently back and forth through the heat. What is happening inside the tube? (As the seed heats up, the moisture inside it escapes as steam and goes to the top and sides of the tube).

7. When the corn pops, blow out the candle and shake the popcorn out.

8. Have the group discuss what changed. Was it fast or slow? Where did the moisture come from? Why did the corn pop? (The moisture is heated and turns to steam, exerting pressure on the outer layer of the kernel. When the outer layer breaks, the corn pops immediately). Ask why some did not pop. (There was a crack in the outer layer and the moisture would have dried already). Is the corn heavier when it is popped?

*COMMENTS:*

Let them try popping with no lid, with more than one kernel in the tube, with different types of corn. Try this with a raisin. (Stop the heating process before the raisin burns). How is this different?

## STEREO HANGERS

*PURPOSE:* Sound travels through metal, string and fingers. Stereo means from two directions at the same time.

*MATERIALS:* 1 roll of thread, 1 metal hanger, two paper cups, and a pencil per child.

*GRADES:* K - 6

*SET-UP:*

1. Ask each child to bring a metal hanger.

2. Build your own stereo hanger first so you know how it works (see diagram).

*PROCEDURE:*

1. Pass out two cups to each child.

2. Cut 2 pieces of thread 1 1/2 feet long. Tie one piece of thread to each end of the hanger. This part is ready. Have them wrap a few inches of the thread around the first joint of the index finger of both hands. Put both fingers into ears and lean over with the hanger dangling down. Tap the hanger gently on a table or other surface, and the vibrations will be heard by each child separately. Have children make sound for each other by running fingers over the thread in patterns.

3. Put a small hole in the middle of the bottom, of the paper cup. String the thread through and tie securely on the inside each cup. Now put the cups up to the ears. (The sounds are much louder).

4. Ask the children to play with the sounds with each other. Let them tap rhythms on the hanger with pencils or other things; tap the hanger over different types of objects. Remove one cup from an ear (no stereo). Have someone hold the thread after the hanger is tapped (the vibration stops, so does the sound).

5. Try tying paper clips to the thread knots inside the cups; does that change the sound? Use another metal object on the strings to test for other possibilities.

6. Discuss how it works. Can they figure it out? (The hanger vibrates when struck, the vibrations travel up the strings, the string vibrating causes the air in the ear to vibrate on the ear drum, producing what each child hears).

*COMMENTS:*

Try to record this with a tape recorder if available. Put the microphone into the cup for best results. Can they make "music"?

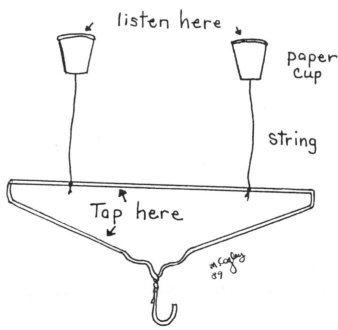

151

## BATTERY CIRCUITS

*PURPOSE:* Familiarity with batteries as electricity, circuits as electrical pathways, bulbs as part of circuits; introduction of "negative and positive poles".

*MATERIALS:* large drawing of a bulb to show group; per group of children-1 D battery, 1 strip of foil 5" X 1" (or electrical thin wire), one 3 volt flashlight bulb, two pieces of masking tape, and a rubber band.

*GRADES:* 2 -6

*SET-UP:*

1. Make the drawing of the bulb in advance, (see diagram).

2. Divide the children into teams.

3. Pass out the materials to each team.

*PROCEDURE:*

1. Ask the children to describe the battery. What is written on it at the top and bottom? Which one says negative and positive? How do you know? What is it made of (cardboard, metal)?. What is a battery used for? Why?

2. Go through the same process with the bulb. Is the small wire (filament) connected to anything?(yes). How is it shaped? Do the large wires touch? Can you see where the larger wires are attached?

3. Tell them to use the materials available and try to make the bulb light up. Draw each attempt, even if it does not work. How many ways can they find that will work? Let an exchange of ideas happen, including failed efforts.

4. Attempts that bypass the bulb, but produce heat on the foil strip will be a "short circuit", and will wear out the battery. Have the children observe that the foil will get hot quickly.

5. Allow enough time and then discuss their efforts. Sharing information is an important part of science. Both successful and failed attempts are valuable learning experiments; discuss them all.

*COMMENTS:*

Make a diagram of what worked and what did not, for use in later experimentation with batteries.

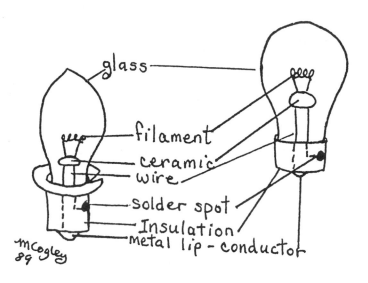

glass

filament

ceramic

wire

solder spot

Insulation

metal lip - conductor

McCogley
89

# INDOOR & OUTDOOR GAMES

Games are a very important part of childhood. Children learn both cooperation and competition through a variety of games in which they participate. Games are best taught with a spirit of fun and sharing rather than competition for winners and losers. Many children play intensely competitive team sports in leagues. The games at an after school program focus attention on skill development, posture, group interaction and willingness to include children who may be less "athletic".

There are many traditional games such as the different forms of tag, four square, dodge ball, jump rope, baseball, and kickball. These games are usually organized and initiated by the children themselves. Certain games are often popular for a length of time, then other games replace them. The following are games which may be adult-initiated. Some are better suited for indoors; others more for outdoors, and some it does not make a difference. Many use nonverbal communication, an important skill for children to learn.

INDOOR & OUTDOOR GAMES

## MOUSE TRAP

*SETTING:* Outdoors or a large indoor space.

*MATERIALS NEEDED:* None

*GRADES:* K-2

*SET-UP:* Nine to twelve children are needed, a larger group can also play.

## WIGGLE WAGGLE CATCH THE TAIL

*SETTING:* Outdoors

*GRADES:* Mixed, younger children can successfully participate.

*MATERIALS NEEDED:* None

*SET-UP:* A minimum of six players, the more the better.

*PROCEDURE:*

1. Choose five to six children to join hands and make a circle. They are the "trap".

2. Choose one player to be the cat and the remaining players to be mice.

3. The "trap" opens and closes by having the children raise and lower their hands. When their hands are raised the trap is open, when their arms are down, the trap is closed.

4. The cat must turn his or her back and count to twenty, while the children who make up the trap open and close the trap.

5. During this time the mice scamper in and out of the trap, being careful not to get caught inside the trap.

6. After counting, the cat quickly turns around and yells SNAP!

7. The children who make up the trap quickly close the trap. All the mice caught inside the trap become part of the trap.

8. This process continues until the last mouse is left. He or she then becomes the cat.

*PROCEDURE:*

1. Players form a line, each player holding the waist of the person in front.

2. The front person is the "head" and the last person the "tail".

3. The "head" tries to catch the "tail" of the line.

4. The children in line must stay holding the waist of the person in front of them (the animal must stay intact).

5. Once the animal breaks apart, the game is stopped and started over.

6. When the "tail" is tagged by the "head", the next person in line becomes the "head" and the former "head" goes to the back, to become the "tail".

## HOOK UP TAG

*SETTING:* Outdoors or a large indoor space.

*GRADES:* 2-6

*MATERIALS NEEDED:* None

*SET-UP:* Ten or more players are needed (an even number of players if possible).

*PROCEDURE:*

1. One player is selected to be "it" and one player is selected to be chased.

2. The other players find a partner to link arms with.

3. The linked pairs arrange themselves in a circle with the "it" player in the middle and the player to be chased on the outside of the circle.

4. The "it" player says "GO" and starts to chase the player on the outside of the circle.

5. The player being chased links up with a pair. At this time he or she yells "GO" and the person on the other end of the pair must detach and run, trying to find another pair to link up with.

6. The "it" player is always trying to tag any player who is not linked up with a pair.

7. When tagged, the person switches places with "it" and begins chasing the other player.

*COMMENTS:*

The players in pairs must remain in a circle, as well as they can.

## STREETS AND ALLEYS

*SETTING:* Outdoors or large indoor space.

*GRADES:* 2-6

*MATERIALS NEEDED:* None

*SET-UP:* This game is best played with a large group, at least 20.

*PROCEDURE:*

1. Choose one child to be the "Cat" and another to be the "Mouse".

2. Have the remaining children stand in even rows of four children or more holding hands and facing forward.

3. Explain that when they are holding hands and facing forward they are in STREET formation. Thus the children make horizontal rows.

4. To make the ALLEYS, they must turn sideways and hold hands with the child in front of and behind them. Thus the children make vertical rows.

5. The teachers repeatedly calls "Streets" and then "Alleys" until the children understand what to do and can change quickly.

6. To begin the game the cat starts inside the front street and the mouse stands inside the back street.

7. The teachers calls "begin" and the cat chases the mouse. Both the cat and mouse must stay inside the streets.

8. After a minute or so, the teacher calls "Alleys", and the children quickly form alleyways. Again the cat and mouse must stay within the alleys.

9. This continues until the cat tags the mouse. At this time two new players are chosen to be cat and mouse.

## COMMENTS:

The words cat and mouse can be changed to anything as long as one clearly chases the other.

## ROCK/SCISSORS/PAPER

*SETTING:* A large space is necessary for this game and it can be played both indoors or out.

*GRADES:* 1 - 6

*MATERIALS NEEDED:* Chalk or tape to make a center line.

*SET-UP:* Two teams are needed.

1. Each team must have a "free zone" designated at opposite ends of the playing area..

2. A center line must be made dividing the two teams.

*PROCEDURE:*

1. Divide the children into two teams. Show them where their "free zone" is located.

2. Each team huddles collectively and decides which symbol they are going to show (rock/scissors/paper).

3. Rock breaks scissors, paper covers rock and scissors cut paper.

4. Once the teams have decided on a sign, they meet at the center line and face each other.

5. At the count of 1-2-3, each team shows their sign.

6. The team that shows the winning symbol chases the losing team, trying to tag as many players as possible. The losing team must run back toward their own free zone, trying not to be tagged.

7. In case of a tie, the teams must go back into a huddle and choose a new symbol.

8. Anyone tagged must join the other team.

## COUNTDOWN

*SETTING:* This game is best played indoors but can be played outdoors.

*GRADES:* 3 -6

*MATERIALS NEEDED:* A blindfold for each participant.

*SET-UP:* A small group, no larger than fifteen.

*PROCEDURE:*

1. All players stand in an enclosed area so that no one will wander off.

2. Have each player wear a blindfold.

3. The trick is not only are the children blindfolded, but

they must not use verbal communication.

4. The leader whispers a number into each participant's ear (if there are ten people, the teacher randomly gives each player a number from 1-10).

5. The children must put themselves into numerical order holding hands without verbal communication. A time limit may be placed on the game so that children unable to find their spot will not become too discouraged.

## ✳ SNAKE PIT

*SETTING:* This game is best for indoors but can be done outdoors.

*GRADES:* 1 - 6

*MATERIALS NEEDED:* Two rattles which can be made from cans or jars with beans or pebbles inside and two blindfolds.

*SET-UP:* This game is best played with 8 or more participants.

*PROCEDURE:*
1. Two players are chosen, one as the pursuer or "it" and one being pursued.

2. The remaining players form a circle called the pit, around the two players.

3. The two players in the middle are blindfolded and are each given a rattle.

4. The object of the game is for "it" to tag the other blindfolded player.

5. For the pursuer to locate the one being pursued, or vice-versa either one must shake their rattle, having the other immediately respond with a shake of his/or her rattle.

6. The key is that the pursuer is allowed only 5 shakes to locate the other player, while the other player can rattle as much as he or she wants or dares to.

7. The job of the other children forming the pit is to insure that the blindfolded players stay inside the circle and they can also help the pursuer keep count of his or her shakes.

## ✳ FRUIT BASKET UPSET

*SETTING:* Indoors

*GRADES:* Mixed, this game can be adapted to meet the age group.

*MATERIALS NEEDED:* A chair for every player.

*SET-UP:* This must be done with at least 12 children.

1. Have the children or teacher write down or draw (for younger children) the name of a fruit (i.e. apples, oranges, bananas, etc.) on a piece of paper, giving at least two people the same fruit.

2. Place the chairs in a circle with one chair in the middle.

3. Explain the rules of the game and stress that there is NO RUNNING!

*PROCEDURE:*
1. One child is picked to be the storyteller.

2. The rest of the children sit down in a chair; there should be one chair for every participant.

3. The storyteller goes around to each child and gives them a piece of paper with the fruit on it.

4. The storyteller sits in the middle and begins to tell a story. When he or she mentions a fruit in the story such as,"and the boy ate an APPLE!" all who were assigned as apples must get up and find another vacant seat, without talking out loud.

5. The storyteller also is trying to find a seat.

6. The person left without a seat sits in the middle and becomes the storyteller.

7. If the storyteller uses the phrase "FRUIT BASKET UPSET!" in the story, then all players must get up and find a new seat.

*COMMENTS:*

There are many variations of this game. Any words can be substituted for fruit such as colors, TV shows, animals, etc.

**CATS AND DOGS**

*SETTING:* In a large space indoors or out.

*GRADES:* K -5

*MATERIALS NEEDED:* Wrapped candy, prizes or other items to be hidden, two large paper or plastic bags.

*SET-UP:*

1. This is best done with a large group of at least 20 children or more.

2. Adults or non-participants must hide the candy or prizes, being careful to have a variety of hiding places with

some very easy to find and others more challenging.

*PROCEDURE:*

1. The children are divided into teams.

2. A leader is chosen for each team and given a bag to collect candy or prizes. (If the groups are very large, two leaders can be chosen or divide into three or more groups.)

3. Each team is given an animal name such as cat or dog.

4. The leaders are the only people allowed to touch the candy.

5. All the cats must meow and point when they locate a piece of candy and the dogs must bark and point to the candy. They may not leave the candy until their leader has picked it up and put it in their bag.

6. If an adult sees a child other than the leader touch a piece of candy, they are out of the game or warned.

7. The leader runs from child to child in their group and picks up the candy. The dog leader may not pick up candy found by a cat and vice-versa.

8. When all the candy is found, the teams form separate circles, count out their candy or prizes and divide them evenly.

*COMMENTS:*

This game makes sure that each child in a team receives equal amount of candy, nuts or small prizes. It is very loud when done indoors!

**MESSAGE HOT POTATO**

*SETTING:* Indoors

*GRADES:* K - 3

*MATERIALS NEEDED:* A small prize, several layers of paper, a pen and tape.

*SET-UP:* This project is best done with a group of 8-15 children.

1. Wrap a small prize in a piece of paper. Then take a slightly larger piece of paper and write out a command such as "say 6

rhyming words," or "run around the circle 3 times," or "spell a five letter word". Wrap and tape the paper with the command around the prize with the writing on the inside. Continue to wrap commands around the prize until there is one command for every child participating.

*PROCEDURE:*

1. Have the children sit in a circle.

2. Explain that each child can only have one turn to unwrap the hot potato and that they must pretend that it is hot!

3. Chant as a group "hot potato, hot potato around you go, where you stop, nobody knows!"

4. The potato is passed quickly around the circle while the children chant. When the chant stops, the person left holding the potato gets to open the paper and do the command. If the child cannot read the message, have an older child read it to them or an adult. If they have had a turn, they must pass it to someone who has not.

5. This continues until the last person opens the prize.

*COMMENTS:*

Records or music of any kind can be substituted for the chant.

## THE DETECTIVE GAME

*SETTING:* Both indoors and outdoors together if possible.

*GRADES:* K - 6

*MATERIALS NEEDED:* Chalk, a magnifying glass (optional)

*SET-UP:* This is best done with at least 20 children.

*PROCEDURE:*

1. Children are divided up into two teams. One team is the "detectives".

2. Each team chooses a captain.

3. The "detectives" team stays in an "off limits area" with the door closed, such as a classroom, for fifteen minutes. The captain of this team carries a magnifying glass.

4. The other team starts off outside the "off limits area" and decides together on a good place to hide. The hiding place must be large enough to fit the entire team. When a place is chosen the group moves towards it. The captain makes chalk arrow s pointing in the direction the team is heading.

5. The team should do some back tracking to try to confuse the detectives. They should also cover as much ground as possible both indoors and out remembering the time limit. The leader must leave arrows every few feet.

6. After fifteen minutes, the detectives look for the other team by following the arrows.

7. When the "detectives" capture the other team, the two teams change places. The second team uses another color of chalk or a different symbol such as wiggly arrows.

*COMMENTS:*

For indoors, rather than chalk to leave clues, other Hansel and Gretel type crumbs can be used such as: lego pieces, checkers, shapes cut out of colored paper, paper clips, and game pieces. For outdoors, bird seed can be substituted for the chalk.

## BURIED TREASURE HUNT

*SETTING:* Indoors and outdoors

*GRADES:* K - 6

*MATERIALS NEEDED:* Prizes, two cardboard boxes, paper, pencils.

*SET-UP:* This works best with a large group of at least 20.

1. Purchase or make prizes for the treasure, making sure there is enough for every participant.

2. Decorate two cardboard boxes to put the treasure inside.

3. Decide where to bury each box of treasure. Each team's treasure box should be hidden in a different place.

4. Adults or older children write down a set of clues for each team. Each clue should lead to the next clue. The clues must be labeled with the teams name and be numbered in sequence of usefulness. The final clue leads to the treasure.

5. Make some clues very easy and others more difficult.

*PROCEDURE:*

1. Divide the children into two teams.

2. Choose a captain of each team, an older child who reads well is best.

3. Explain the game and that they must work together to find the treasure.

4. See which team finds the treasure first.

5. When the treasure has been found, each child receives a prize out of the box.

*COMMENTS:*

For smaller groups only one treasure box can be used.

## A SPOOK HOUSE

A haunted house can be an exciting part of a celebration. Design your house with whatever you have handy, it does not have to be fancy or large. Please make sure that fearful children are allowed the option to NOT enter.

*SUGGESTIONS FOR HAUNTING:*

1. Create the sections of the house based on what children are planning to wear. A mad scientist, mummy, or witch work well inside the house. Dancers, French maids, punks and "cool dudes" are great tour guides through the house.

2. Engineer "rooms" by using large sheets of material, rope, pins, and curtains fastened together. Large cardboard sheets can also be walls. Paint them black. Long, thin cardboard boxes make wonderful coffins or sarcophagi, especially edged in gold spray paint.

3. Make tunnels with appliance boxes painted black. They can have odd things on the floor such as: rug bits, styrofoam chips, packing parts, ropes, balloons. Crepe paper or yarn can be hung off the ends to form an eerie texture on faces as children crawl through.

4. Yarn can be strung from curtains and tops of cardboard for a creepy feeling. Spider webs can be strung from yarn across entrances.

5. Classic spooky stuff like grapes for eyes and spaghetti for brains are a lot of fun but very frightening for some children, and messy to clean up.

6. The entrance and exit are important. Design door ways that are unique. A slide out into piles of balloons is an exciting finish.

7. Place children helpers strategically around the inside of the house. Provide them with flashlights or muted lights to highlight their faces, costumes, or actions.

8. Have things that swing down from the ceiling and get pulled back and forth across a walking area. Use a rope and a hidden child for this.

9. Music is a very important part of the effect. Use spooky, scary sounds or music. These can be bought or created by the children making the house. Have a tape that is long enough, or a child placed to aim the speakers and replay the tape.

10. Send children through the house in small groups escorted by a child with a flashlight.

11. Fluorescent paint is a wonderful decoration and fans make "spirit winds."

12. Be creative and have fun!

# RESOURCES

## School-Age Care General Information

Arns, B. *Survival Guide: to School-Age Child Care.* Huntington Beach CA: School-Age Workshops Press, 1988. (School-Age Workshop Press, PO Box 5012, Huntington Beach CA 92615)

Baden, et al. *School-Age Child Care: An Action Manual.* Wellesley MA: School-Age Child Care Project, 1982.(School-Age Child Care Project, Wellesley College Center for Research on Women, Wellesley MA 02181)

Bender, et al. *Half a Childhood - Time for School-Age Child Care.* Nashville Tn: School-Age NOTES, 1984. (School-Age NOTES, PO Box 40205, Nashville TN 37204)

Bergstrom, J. *School's Out—Now What?* Berkeley CA: Ten Speed Press, 1984.

Blau, R., et al. *Activities for School-Age Child Care: Playing and Learning, Rev. Ed.* Washington DC: National Association for the Education of Young Children, 1989. (NAEYC, 1834 Connecticut Blvd. N.W., Washington DC 20009)

California Child Care Initiative. *School-Age Child Care Getting It Started in Your Community.* San Francisco: 1986. (Available from California Child Care Resource and Referral Network, 111 New Montgomery, 7th Floor, San Francisco, CA 94105, 415-882-0234)

Child Care Information Exchange *#101 School Age Day Care.* PO Box 2890, Redmond WA 98073.

Cohen, A. *School-Age Child Care: A Legal Manual For School Administrators.* San Francisco: Child Care Law Center 1984. (Child Care Law Center, 22 2nd St. 5th Fl., San Francisco CA 94105)

Diffendal, E. *Day Care for School-Age Children.* Washington DC: UNCO, Inc., 1973.

Elkind, D. *The Hurried Child.* Reading MA: Addison Wesley Publishing Co., 1988.

Fink, D. *School-Age Children With Special Needs: What Do They Do When School Is Out?* Boston: Exceptional Parent Press, 1988. (Available from School-Age NOTES)

Greenman, J. *Caring Spaces, Learning Places: Children's Environments that Work.* Redmond WA: Exchange Press, 1988. (Available from School-Age NOTES)

Hawkins, N. & Vandergriff, B. *Caring for School-Age Children: A Church Program Guide.* Nashville TN: Convention Press, 1986. (Available from School-Age NOTES)

Long, T. & Long, L. *The Handbook for Latchkey Children and Their Parents.* New York: Arbor House, 1983.

Military Child Care Project. *Caring for School-Age Children.* Washington DC: Superintendent of Documents, U.S. Government Printing Office, 1980.

Musson, S. & Gibbons, M. *The New Youth Challenge: A Model for Working with Older Children in School-Age Child Care.* Nashville TN: School-Age NOTES, 1988. (PO Box 40205, Nashville TN 37204)

Prescott, E. & Milich, C. *School's Out! Group Day Care for the School-Age Child.* Pasadena CA: Pacific Oaks College, 1974.

Prescott, E. & Milich, C. *School's Out! Family Day Care for the School-Age Child.* Pasadena CA: Pacific Oaks College, 1975.

Ranson, L. & Salisbury Hedges, P. *Program Development for School-Age Children Caregiver Book and Trainer's Guide.* Stillwater OK: Child Care Careers, Inc., 1989. (Child Care Careers, Inc. HEW 032, Oklahoma State University, Stillwater OK 74078, 405-744- 5060)

163

Reider, B. *A Hooray Kind of Kid: A Child's Self-Esteem and How to Build It*. El Dorado Hills CA: Sierra House Publishing, 1988.

Southeastern Pennsylvania Child Care Project, *"School-Age Care: Addressing A Crisis"* Regional Conference, May 5, 1988. (Book available through Southeastern PA School-Age Child Care Project, Day Care Association of Montgomery Co., 601 Knight Road, Ambler PA 19002)

Wessler, M. & Sausman, T. *Caring for Children Before and After School*. Wauwatosa, WI: Siebert Lutheran Foundation, 1986.

**General Arts And Crafts And Activity Books**

Bergstrom, J. & Bergstrom, C. *All the Best Contests for Kids*. Berkeley CA: Ten Speed Press, 1988. (Available from School-Age NOTES)

Blau, R., et al. *Activities for School-Age Child Care: Playing and Learning, Rev. Ed.* Washington DC: National Association for the Education of Young Children, 1989.

Bodger, L. *Woman's Day Dough Crafts*. New York: Sedgewood Press, 1983.

Cole, A., et al. *A Pumpkin in a Pear Tree*. Boston: Little, Brown & Co., 1976.

Croft, D. *Recipes For Busy Little Hands*. San Francisco CA.: R & E Associates, 1973.

Frank, M. *I Can Make a Rainbow!* Nashville TN: Incentive Publishing, 1976. (Available from School-Age NOTES)

Haas, C. *The Big Book of Fun*. Chicago: Chicago Review Press, 1987. (Available from School-Age NOTES)

Haas, C. & Friedman, A. *My Own Fun - Activities for Kids Ages 7- 12*. Chicago: Chicago Review Press, 1990 (Available from School-Age NOTES)

Highlights Creative Crafts Series. *132 Gift Crafts Kids Can Make & 127 Anytime Crafts Kids Can Make*. Columbus OH: Highlights for Children, 1981.

Kohl, M. *Scribble Cookies*. Bellingham WA: Bright Ring Publishing, 1985.

_____ *Mudworks: Creative Clay, Dough, and Modeling Experiences for Children*. Bellingham WA: Bright Ring Publishing, 1989.

Marzollo, J. *Superkids Creative Learning Activities for Children 5-15*. New York: Harper & Row, Publishers, 1981.

Renfro, N. *Puppets and the Art of Story Creation*. Austin TX: Nancy Renfro Studios, 1979.

_____ *Bags are Big!* Austin TX: Nancy Renfro Studios, 1986.

Robinson, J. *Activities for Anyone, Anytime, Anywhere*. Boston: Little, Brown & Co., 1983.

Rogovin, A. *Let Me Do It!* New York: Thomas Y. Crowell, Publishers, 1980.

Roufberg, R. *The Kitchen Crafts Workshop*. New York: Butterick Publishing, 1976.

Stangl, Jean. *Magic Mixtures*. Belmont CA: Fearon Teacher Aids, David S. Lake Publishers, 1986.

**Multicultural**

Bernstein, B. & Blair, L. *Native American Crafts Workshop*. Belmont CA: Pitman Learning, Inc., 1982. (Available from School-Age NOTES)

Cole, A. et al. *Children are Children are Children*. Boston: Little, Brown & Co., 1978.

Derman-Sparks, L. *Anti-Bias Curriculum - Tools for Empowering Young Children*. Washington DC: National Association for the Education of Young Children, 1989.

Kendall, F. *Diversity in the Classroom*. New York: Teachers College Press, 1983.

Lee, N. & Oldham, L. *Hands On Heritage*. Long Beach CA: Hands on Publications, 1978.

Newsome, A. *Crafts and Toys from Around the World*. New York: Julian Messner, 1972.

Schuman, J. *Art From Many Hands - Multi-Cultural Art Projects*. Worcester MA: Davis Publications Inc., 1981.

Temko, Florence. *Folk Crafts for World Friendship*. New York: Doubleday, 1976.

**Science**

Allison, L. and Katz, D. *Gee Wiz: How to Mix Art and Science or The Art of Thinking Scientifically*. Boston: Little, Brown & Co., 1982. (Available from School-Age NOTES)

Cobb, V. *Science Experiments You Can Eat*. New York: Lippincott, 1973.

_____ & Darling, K. *Bet You Can*. New York: Avon Books, 1983.

Herbert, D. *Mr. Wizards's Supermarket Science*. New York: Random House, 1980

_____ *Mr. Wizard's 400 Experiments in Science*. New Jersey: Ruchlis Book Lab, 1968.

Stein, S. *The Science Book*. New York: Workman Publishing, 1979.

Strongin, H. *Science on a Shoe String*. Menlo Park CA: Addison-Wesley Publishing Co., 1985.

Tunheim, J. and Branum, J. *Science and Physics Education for Early Childhood Teachers and Their Young Children*. Not yet published, available through, Business and Education Institute, Dakota State College, Madison, SD 57042.

Western Association of Fish and Wildlife Agency and Western Regional Environmental Education Council. *Project Wild (Elementary)*. Salina Star Route, Boulder CO 80302, 1983.

Williams, R., Rockwell, R. & Sherwood, E. *Mudpies to Magnets*. Mt. Rainier MD: Gryphon House, 1987. (Available from School-Age NOTES)

Zubrowski, B. *Children's Museum Activity Books, Ball Point Pens; Bubbles; Milk Carton Blocks*. Boston: Little, Brown & Co., 1979.

**Planting And Nature Crafts**

Allison, L. *The Reasons for the Seasons*. Boston: Little, Brown & Co., 1985.

Cole, A, Haas, C. & Naftzger, B. *Backyard Vacation*. Boston: Little, Brown & Co., 1980.

Cramblit, J and Loebel, J. *Flowers are For Keeping*. New York: Julian Messner, 1979.

Forte, I. & Frank, M. *Puddles and Wings and Grapevine Swings*. Nashville TN: Incentive Publications, 1982. (Available from School-Age NOTES)

Kane, J. *Art Through Nature*. Homes Beach FL: Learning Publications, 1985.

Rockwell et. al, *Hug A Tree*. Mt. Rainier MD: Gryphon House, Inc., 1983.

Sisson, E. *Nature With Children of All Ages*. Englewood Cliffs NJ: Prentice-Hall, Inc., 1982.

*The Beautiful Naturecraft Book*. New York: Sterling Publishing Co, Inc., 1979.

**Circle Time Activities, Records, Music, And Creative Dramatics**

Berman, Marsha and Barlin, Ann. (Record) *Dance a Story. Sing a Song*. Available through Learning Through Movement, 5757 Ranchito, Van Nuys CA 91419

Capon, J. *Basic Movement Activities*. Belmont CA: Fearon Teacher Aides, David S. Lake, 1975.

Nelson, Esther. *The Silly Songbook, The Funny Songbook, The Fun-To-Sing Songbook, Worlds Best Funny Songs, Everybody Sing & Dance.* Cassettes and songbooks available through Dimension 5 Box 403 - Kingsbridge Station, Bronx NY 10463 (212)-548-6112

Oldfield, M. *More Tell and Draw Stories.* Creative Story Time Publishers, 1969.

Olson, M. *Tell and Draw Stories.* Creative Story Time Publishers, 1963.

Patrick, K., Gift, C. & Bearden, L. (Record) *Monsters and Monstrous Things.* Nashville TN: UpbeatBasics 1983.

Plum City Players. (Record) *The Dinosaur Fiskrs'* Choice Records 1450 Sixth St. Berkeley CA 94710.

Raven, Nancy. (Record) *The House We Live In Vol II.* Pacific Cascade Records 47534 McKenzie Hwy., Vida OR 97488.

Rosenberg, H. *Creative Drama and Imagination.* Holt, Rinehart, and Winston, 1987.

Walther, T. *Make Mine Music.* Boston: Little, Brown, and Co. 1981. (Available from School-Age NOTES)

## Games

Cihak, M. & Heron, B. *Games Children Should Play.* Santa Monica CA: Goodyear Publishing Co., 1980.

Fluegelman, A (Ed). *The New Games Book.* Garden City NJ: The New Games Foundation, Doubleday & Company, 1976.

_____*More New Games.* Garden City NJ, Dolphin Books, Doubleday & Company, 1981.

Gregson, B. *The Incredible Indoors Game Book* and *The Outrageous Outdoor Games Book.* Belmont CA: David S. Lake Publishers, 1982. (Available from School-Age NOTES)

Hall, Sweeny and Esser. *Until the Whistle Blows.* Santa Monica CA: Goodyear Publishing, 1977.

Michaelis, D & B. *Learning Through Noncompetitive Activities and Play.* Palo Alto CA: 1977. (Available from School-Age NOTES)

Orlick, T. *The Cooperative Sports and Games Book.* New York: Pantheon Books, 1978.

_____*The Second Cooperative Sports and Games Book.* New York: Pantheon Books, 1982.

Pearson, C. *Make your Own Games Workshop.* Belmont CA: David S. Lakes Publishers, 1982.

Skolnik, P. *Jump Rope!* New York: Workman Publishing Co., 1974.

Therrell, J. *How to Play with Kids.* Pacifica CA: Play Today Press, 1989. (Available from School-Age NOTES)

## Older Children And Early Adolescents

*After-School Programs: What Works and Why (Videotape) and Early Adolescent Sexuality: Resources for Professionals, Parents and Young Adolescents.* (Resource list) 1989. Center for Early Adolescence, 1982. Available from the University of North Carolina at Chapel Hill, Suite 211, Carr Mill Mall, Carrboro, NC, 27510, (919)-966-1148

Children's Defense Fund. *Opportunities For Prevention: Building After-School and Summer Programs for Young Adolescents.* Publication of the Adolescent Pregnancy Prevention Clearinghouse, 1987. (Available from: Publications, Children's Defense Fund, 122 C Street, N.W. Washington DC 20001, $4.50)

Devault, C. & Strong, B. *Christy's Chance, Danny's Dilemma, Serena's Secret*. Santa Cruz CA: Network Publications, 1987.

Early Adolescent Helper Program, Center for Advanced Study in Education (CASE). *Child Care Helper Program: A Guide for Teachers and Program Leaders*. 1984. (Available from: CASE/Helper Program, 25 West 43rd St. Rm 620, New York NY 10036, (212)-642- 2947)

Lefstein, L. & Lipsitz, J. *3:00-6:00 P.M.: Programs for Young Adolescents*. Center for Early Adolescence, 1986. (Available from the University of North Carolina at Chapel Hill, Suite 211, Carr Mill Mall, Carrboro NC 27510, 919-966-1148)

Lefstein, L. et al. *3:00 to 6:00 P.M.: Young Adolescents at Home and in the Community*. Center for Early Adolescence, 1982.

Musson, S. & Gibbons, M. *The New Youth Challenge: A Model for Working with Older Children in School-Age Child Care*. Nashville TN: School-Age NOTES, 1988. (Available from School-Age NOTES)

## Problem Solving, Social Problem Solving And Conflict Resolution

Anderson & Bereite. *Thinking Games Books 1 & 2*. Belmont CA: Pitman Learning, Inc., 1980.

Carnow, G. *Prolific Thinkers Guide to Prolific Thinking*. Los Angeles: Prolific Thinkers, 1984. (To purchase write to Prolifica Thinkers, 5453 E. Beverly Blvd., Los Angeles, CA. 90022)

Charles, R., Mason, R. and Martin, L. *Problem Experiences in Mathematics*. Menlo Park CA: Addison Wesley Publishing Co., 1985.

Cherry, C. *Please Don't Sit on the Kids*. Belmont CA: David S. Lake Publishers, 1983. (Available from School-Age NOTES)

Crary, E. *Kids Can Cooperate: A Practical Guide to Teaching Problem Solving*. Seattle WA: Parenting Press, 1979.

Dolan, D. *Teaching Problem-Solving Strategies*. Menlo Park CA: Addison Wesley Publishing Co., 1983.

Gibbs, J. *TRIBES*. Santa Rosa CA: Center-Source Publications, 1987. (PO Box 436, Santa Rosa CA 95402)

Gourley, T. & Micklus, S. *Problems, Problems, Problems*. Glassboro NJ: Creative Competitions, 1984. (305 Tesconi Cir., Glassboro NJ 08028)

Harnadek, A. *Figure Patterns*. Pacific Grove CA: Midwest Publications, 1979. (Available from Critical Thinking Press, PO Box 448, Pacific Grove CA 93950)

Harnadek, A. *Inferences A & B*. Pacific Grove CA: Midwest Publications, 1979.

Harnadek, A. *Patterns*. Pacific Grove CA: Midwest Publications, 1977.

Hester, J. and Killian, D. *Cartoons for Thinking: Issues in Ethics and Values*. Monroe NY: Trillium Press.

Kreidler, W. *Creative Conflict Resolution*. Glenview IL: Scott Foresman and Co., 1984.

Levy, N. & Melchior, T. *Stories to Stretch the Mind*. Monroe NY: Trillium Press, Revised Addition 1989 (Trillium Press, PO Box 209, Monroe NY 10950)

*Mathematics Framework K-12*. Sacramento CA: California State Department of Education, 1985.

Micklus, S. *Odyssey of the Mind*. Glassboro NJ: Creative Competitions, 1987. Odyssey of the Mind Training Packet. Write for information and competition applications to PO Box 27, Glassboro NJ 08028.

Meyer, Carol and Sallee, Tom. *Make it Simpler*. Menlo Park CA: Addison Wesley Pub. Co., 1983.

Post, E. & Cads, S. *LOGIC ANYONE?*. Belmont CA: David S. Lakes Publishers, 1982.

*Problem Parade*. Palo Alto CA: Dale Seymour Publications (PO Box 10888, Palo Alto CA 94303)

*Thinkercises.*, a series of thinking explorations from Kolbe Concepts, PO Box 15050, Phoenix AZ 85060.

## Publications, Catalogs, Organizations And Newsletters

Afterschool Catalog, 1401 John Street, Manhattan Beach CA 90266 - (213)-545-5437

California School-Age Consortium, CSAC Review, 70 10th St., Ste. 201, San Francisco CA 94103, (415)-621-4594

Child Care Information Exchange (The Director's Magazine), P.O. Box 2890, Redmond WA 98073

Day Care for School Agers. (Publication # 0957) Child Care Program, Texas Department of Human Services, P.O. Box 149030 MC523-E, Austin, TX 78714-9030.

National Association for the Education of Young Children (NAEYC), Young Children, Annual Conference, Informational Services, Books Posters, Brochures, and Videos. 1834 Connecticut Ave. N.W., Washington DC 20009, (202)-232-8777 or (800)-424-2460

School-Age NOTES. (Newsletter for School-Age Care Professionals and a national resource organization on school-age care) P.O. Box 40205, Nashville TN 37204, (615)-242-8464

The National School-Age Child Care Alliance. Contact Ellen Gannett, SACC Project, Wellesley College Center for Research on Women, Wellesley MA 02181 - (617)-431-1453

Wellesley College School-Age Child Care Project, Wellesley College Center for Research on Woman, Wellesley MA 02181 (617)- 431-1453